Guidebook to the Future

Practical Advice for a Changing World

By Candace Caddick

Brightstone Publishing

First published 2013

Published by Brightstone Publishing
2 High Trees Road
Reigate, Surrey RH2 7EJ
United Kingdom

ISBN registered to me, the author, under Brightstone Publishing.

British Library Cataloguing in Publication Data
A catalogue record for this book is available from the British Library

ISBN 978-0-9565009-3-9

Printed in the United Kingdom

Cover image: Lydford Gorge, Devon, UK

With Gratitude to my daughter Pippa Caddick for her generous help

Books by Candace Caddick

Planet Earth Today: How the Earth and Humanity Developed Together and Where We're Going Next (April 2010)

The Downfall of Atlantis: A History of the Tragic Events Leading to Catastrophe (February 2011)

And I Saw a New Earth: 2012 and Beyond (May 2012)

Guidebook to the Future: Practical Advice for a Changing World   (May 2013)

Contents

Scientific Discoveries and Changes in Travel

Acknowledgements

This book would not have been possible without the help of my daughter Pippa who copy-edited the manuscript on train journeys in and out of London, and my other daughter Heather who learned the typesetting and cover design software necessary for publication. I also appreciate the help and encouragement of my friends Reiki Master Jean Jones, Gill Hancock, Beth Carson and Alison Hopkins. The Reiki Association UK community has also been very supportive. Having friends and a community behind me with their support keeps me writing.

Introduction

This is a channelled book about change, by the Archangels who make up the Archangelic Collective. We share a common angelic soul and purpose. In the past the Collective divided into separate beings so as to communicate our teachings more easily. Earth-time has no effect on us and we are able to see your past, present and future. We wish to guide and help you to look forward with happy anticipation to this new 26,000 year galactic cycle.

What kind of changes can be expected on Earth in the first years of the new cycle? In December 2012 the Earth was reborn in a manner that allowed her to subtly change her personality and alter the way she relates to humanity. Earth is now a planet that intends to look after herself as well as her guests, and she will be providing the conditions to bring the current game to an end. The goal for humanity is to ascend together along with the Earth and continue learning as a soul of light at a higher level. From the early months of 2013 each new change will occur at an ever-accelerating rate.

People do not often like radical change, but what if new events lead to a fairer world where you live in greater contentment? In this book we (the angelic authors) are trying to reassure you that change can happen fast, and can be very beneficial. In fact, the more you are able to accept new changes the quicker you may enjoy a satisfying life. We want to help everyone move forward to happiness without fear about what the future will bring.

One of the biggest changes to take place in 2013 was the dissolution of the energy shell around the Earth in late winter. This allowed humanity and Earth to reconnect to the rest of the universe and to learn from the other life present there. The energy shell kept both you and the Earth isolated for long ages. It is such a fundamental event to move from isolation to reconnection that this will drive forward many changes in your lives. We write to prepare you and to help you rethink issues such as the energy behind the way your food is grown, rapid change in finance and societies, and the way you live with animals. These are exciting times and we want to help you enjoy them.

We are pleased to be in direct contact with you again.

The Archangelic Collective

Getting the Most from Life on the New Earth

1

Rediscovering Happiness

2013 IS THE first year of the new Earth, and it's a year that will take you by surprise. We are angels of love and light and we wished to write this book to guide you during the coming years of rapid change. Our previous books through this channel were written to tell the story of humanity right up to this point in history. This book is to help you chose a pathway that will lead you to happiness. We angels believe there is nothing greater than happiness; it is an aspect of light. It is the one item that is worth having, and we can see you as a shining ball of light when you are happy. When you are unhappy and stressed, you do not shine and to our eyes appear grey, and this makes it harder to see you energetically. Too many of you are accustomed to feeling unhappy and stressed.

Happiness is available to everyone, but very few of you now remember how to live joyfully. You have been misled into finding your personal happiness by false ideas, and many of you have come to believe that you can buy it with money.

Because happiness is the energetic equivalent of love, it's the same as saying you can buy real love. Often this kind of happiness comes at other people's expense and leads to a personal, instead of global, view of joy. It's not possible for you to be the one happy person in a crowd of unhappy people because you don't exist in isolation. The despair of those who you live among creates an atmosphere of sadness, and you can't escape it even if you pretend it has nothing to do with you, and you can't block it out of your lives. The sadness of every person on the planet affects every other person because you are all one. When you are happy or laughing your joy spreads and helps everyone else to be happy and joyful. Emotions are a part of your individual environment and they shape the environment in the rest of the world. Emotions contain a lot of energy.

It was once easier for you to be happy every day when you did not base your happiness on material things. But you saw advertisements for beautiful objects and read the celebrity gossip about wealthy extravagance, and if only you had the same possessions and lifestyles as they did you would be happy. You did not see that often another's wealth came by drawing everyone else's money into their own pockets while the gap between the haves and have-nots widened. You were told a number of lies about money, taxes and wealth that allowed others to collect more money than they needed in order to live. In the past the best warrior was king, and his closest friends were ennobled; between them they collected all the property for themselves. Now you have another group of people collecting for themselves while the old nobility has, for the most part, managed to hang onto their property. This is the real economics which is both ignored and terribly serious for the rest of you, and it has been happening on Earth for millennia. It was once accepted by established societies that the wealthiest made their money from the work of their employees or slaves, but why should some work be rewarded at a rate that starves others?

Do you think the way money is accumulated is imbalanced? Or do you accept it as simply a fact of life? What is a fair reward for a day of manual work or, on the other hand, for carrying the full responsibility of a company? Currently the CEO of a large company in the USA earns around four hundred and seventy-five times the amount of an employee. We can contrast what is happening to people these days with bees; where every bee has a job and a purpose. No bee is rewarded above the other bees, and each has his part to play in the life of the hive. The queen bee does not rule her hive, she lives simply to lay eggs and keep the colony alive. Bees are one of the species that choose to use its single soul in closer connection than some other life forms. When scientists wonder how bees communicate the location of pollen so effectively, they cannot conceive of a bee form of telepathy. Bees are many bodies with one mind and do not have to physically express what they are thinking, as you do by talking.

The human population has enough members to maintain its existence and each person has a different role to play in daily life. In this case humanity does not work together, in the way each bee works to keep the hive alive. Some people behave like one bee with a large vat of honey who will not share it even when it is unable to eat it all. Humanity has arrived at this position and if you take the analogy further you will see the dead bees accumulating in the bottom of the hive from starvation while some have more honey than they can eat. This book is about the unity of the single human soul, and how if you have starved your brothers then you have starved yourself.

Humanity is a soul group that deliberately divided into numerous splinters and your existence here on Earth is to learn what it is to be a tiny part of the whole of Creation. While alive you undergo many experiences and have the opportunity to learn all about life and your place in the universe. Your short lives are fragments of a greater existence and over the course of your many lives you slowly piece together knowledge about who you really are. You are more than a single person with one life. You are a piece of the greater human soul, one of the brightest, most creative and much-loved souls in the universe. Humanity has a long history of previous experiences on other planets where you already learned that you are a small part of the Creator. You are here on Earth learning it all over again under a new set of circumstances. This time you thought about how difficult you could make the learning experience and ran straight into a set-back in Atlantis.

Humanity is playing an extended game of 'Can we find God from a position of complete unknowing?' Against all the odds, many of you have managed to do exactly that. When God created the universes He chose to divide Himself into many small pieces in order to experience life and get to know Himself. The human soul was one of those small pieces and then divided seven billion times to make the number of humans living on Earth at the moment. As a basic condition of the game, you chose to forget that you were all one, and even when you die your own soul rests at the level of understanding it has achieved while alive. After death you take the knowledge you acquired and add it to what you previously learned from living, and in this way slowly accumulate an understanding of your soul's purpose here. This is unique to humanity, as other souls are not separate from one another in life or death. If you have a pet you love, that pet will be reborn in the same species one day, but it will have all the knowledge that each member of it species has learned each time it is alive While you learn as a single being, they learn by pooling their knowledge together, especially once they are dead. They rejoin their soul group and the knowledge of the soul group become assimilated by each of them. The living pet can access this knowledge, but it depends on the animal how easy it is for them to do so. Bees and wolves are very connected inside their species, but cats for example, do not choose to connect so closely to each other whilst alive.

You also chose during your lifetimes here to be blind to the higher dimensions, and you are unable to see higher-dimensional beings such as angels. You only see three dimensions at this point, but you have the ability now to interact with five dimensions: height, width, depth, time and the elementals (fairies, unicorns, dragons, etc.). You chose not to share the close contact of a school of fish or a flock of birds. By learning as individuals you have produced a few teachers of great wisdom and these are now the human ascended masters. They are human and their wisdom is present as part of the greater human soul. Under extremely difficult conditions these men and women were able to learn once again that they are a tiny part of God. Now they exist (for the most part) in spirit form, and will help you if asked. After lifetimes spent learning, they put together the knowledge of the true nature of their existence.

One day all of humanity will remember its role in the universe and recombine as a single soul. Until that time the wisdom of the few ascended masters is available to help the rest of you move forward; they can lead you, and even though they are dead, their souls are not gone. The existence of these masters draws the rest of you towards the light. They keep travelling forward and the rest of you hurry to catch up. A soul group works together whether the members are living or dead. Because you are one soul, all members of your soul group will have to come to the same level of realisation before humanity ascends. This will happen at different speeds because of the way you divided into individuals.

Humanity has been part of an interconnecting set of games orchestrated by the sentient planet Earth. She agreed to host humanity in a risky game to give you the opportunity to find God once more, one in which you were unable to see the higher dimensions. Your ability to be aware of the angels and demons around you currently depends on small things like the hairs rising on the backs of your necks, or a strong feeling that you shouldn't go down a certain path. Animals can simply see all the dimensions and avoid any beings they wish. On other planets the population can see angels and demons and choose whether they interact with them or not. You have very little choice in the matter of demons, and many of you don't believe they exist. Demons are angels of darkness, and the authors of this book are angels of light. We are all one family of beings, and play out our assigned roles to the best of our ability and learn alongside of you.

The human soul and its relationship to the Earth is the subject of our previous books *Planet Earth Today*, *The Downfall of Atlantis*, and *And I Saw A New Earth*. The final part of the last-mentioned book describes the speed of the end of the universe once humanity remembers that it is part of

God. The plan is for humanity to join together with the Earth and the other souls living here in ascension, and become one large soul of light sharing knowledge and experiences. It will be the largest ball of light in this universe and it will change the balance, tipping it back from dark to light before the universe itself is drawn back into God.

After any ascension, the soul does not come to an end. It continues to learn under a different set of circumstances. There is no point in stopping the process of learning about yourselves and the greater universe. The fastest learning takes place while living on a planet, but there are souls who have never incarnated and they learn by their interactions with those with physical bodies. The lessons learned by not being incarnate are as valuable as the many lessons learned while alive on a planet, but they are different. When all the lessons are learned we tell our stories to God and rejoin Him in love.

This particular planetary ascension was arranged so that all who are here, people, planet, elementals, insects and animals, etc. will ascend together. Knowledge, experience and light will be combined into one very large soul group. If you join together with others you have begun a process that will end when you return to God, and are one with Him again.

2012 was the final year of the old Earth before she was exposed to the light of the Central Sun, when she received a boost in energy and renewed herself for another 26,000 year cycle. During the previous few thousand years you rode quietly on the back of a quiescent planet, but after the rebirth of the Earth it will be like a wild ride on the back of a tiger. What effect will this have on you? You have to be ready for everything to change, perhaps suddenly, and those who have let go their preconceptions, old habits, and unnecessary material possessions will find their ride the easiest. What has worked for you in the old world will not necessarily work for you in the new. You may have to be ready to emigrate, or perhaps you are in exactly the right place. Many of you spend a lot of time looking after your possessions whether they are used regularly or not, and there are more enjoyable ways to spend your time. Let go of the unnecessary, and be ready to move forward quickly.

There is bodily stress involved in being in the wrong place and the wrong job. If you have reached a stressful point in your lives, it is preferable to make the effort to change. Changing to a life you love in 2013 will make you happy and you will wonder why it took you so long. It requires a firm belief that changes are not bad, and that it is possible to change to something better. You will have to make the effort and make the changes yourselves, and if you look around you see many are doing exactly that. It is easier to walk through your life if you are not overburdened. We see many of you walking forward with your arms full of unnecessary beliefs and possessions, when you could lay them down and walk unencumbered. It is safe for you to do so, and you will be able to take advantage of new opportunities more easily and be more flexible. You may find yourself trudging along right now but in the future you can skip and hop without hindrance.

We can not emphasize this enough; there will be changes and you will value flexibility over solid wealth. For thousands of years you have sought security by accumulating wealth and working for sizeable houses or bank balances. How can this change so suddenly and what is going to happen to people who have a lot of money and want to pass it on to their heirs? What would seem fast to you: a generation, a year, five years? There is no cut off date for the end of accumulated wealth, but the energy will no longer support extremes of inequality. The top and bottom of the economic scale will draw together as the top collapses. At the moment wealth is built on a lot of energy that supports its vast size. Even as you stand upright you are supported by energy, and when you are tired you sit down. Withdrawing Earth energy will cause the steady reduction of the greatest stockpiles of money and they will not be supported in being rebuilt in the same manner. Will you lend someone else your own energy so they can enrich themselves?

The planet has the ability to run its own life and make its own choices. Once she entered into a contract with you she agreed to certain conditions for the duration of your time here, and she abides by these rules. When the game began she provided a paradise world for you where crops grew easily, rain and sunshine were balanced, as were heat and cold. You understood your own obligations and responsibilities to her and to all other life forms here as her guests. Humanity came to learn about their relationship to their Creator, and as a wise old soul of light the Earth would not harm any of her guests. Today you find yourselves still here with some repairs to make and cleaning up to do. To be fair, you did not come here to cause damage to a planet or extinction to other soul groups. You were deceived and too blind to see through fog into reality. Because you could not see the higher dimensions you never saw the whole story. There are twelve dimensions of which you see three, and your entire societies have been built on those three dimensions or on one-quarter of reality. Truly, as Plato once wrote, you have been watching reality in the movement of shadows on the cave wall, and never looked away from the wall to reality. You believed you were seeing the truth when it was just a shadow. Those days of half-truth and lies are over, and it's time to look away and see the colours and reality of the new world you live on.

The way to discover truth is to use your heart to assess people and situations in daily life. This can sound a bit scary and unnecessary as you have a brain, but the soul is accessible through the heart and the brain is the servant of the soul. Your individual soul is far wiser with many lifetimes of experience than your brain will ever be in one lifetime. Sometimes you can listen to a politician and realise their hearts are not engaged. They are telling you whatever they think will impress you, a little speech that will tick all the boxes and disguise any real feelings in case they lose your vote. If you can see this far into a speech then you can see how you are being tricked. Those who give speeches in this way are not aware of their own hearts or the purpose of their own soul. Humans have been so unkind to each other in the past that most people guard their hearts very carefully so they won't be hurt again. We are asking you to open up your hearts and be brave. A person who is in touch with their soul is the strongest type of person on the planet. More than that, they can show others that it is safe to speak with passion from the heart.

Speaking from the heart will reach out and touch others. A heart of love and light does not lie, and others will recognise the truth when it's spoken. We are talking about making changes by speaking from the one place where you can trust that you are connected to the truth. When you listen to someone who is passionate about what they say then you have the pleasure of being spoken to with truth from their heart. It's insulting to be lied to all the time and hedged about with so many falsehoods you can barely make an informed decision.

We can see your hearts because they shine with the light of love, but sometimes hearts emit no light at all and are grey and colourless. Whether you are one of those who love romantically or platonically, love your God or love others, you are easy for us to see when you emit love and warmth. When someone is a bright spark or flame, or shines brightly we are able to see them on the face of the Earth. People carry different amounts of light, and when you hear a phrase such as 'don't hide your light under a bushel', or 'let your light shine' it is referring to the love in your hearts shining forth and making a difference.

In a crowd of people there are a wide variety of lights shining outwards, but many people's hearts are so grey they seem to exist fearfully and without love. Others are beginning to shine more now, while there are some whose brightness makes them very easy to find. If you take one bright person who is not afraid to show their love and shine, they do not run short of love by sharing it with others. Some of those whose hearts are just beginning to shine have learned about love by being in the presence of these people, and begin to relax and shine light themselves. In this way the light of love spreads from heart to heart, and little fires are rekindled in humanity. This does not need to happen slowly as you are all born with the ability to love.

Those people who appear grey are not lost causes, as they are born with the ability to love just like any other human being. The example of the Budda is relevant here; as a wealthy young man he did not emit much light until he meditated and became enlightened. As the Budda he blazed forth in a way that must have astonished his early companions. The word 'enlightened' is exactly the right word to describe the process a person goes through to emit high levels of light. One is taught by experiencing love, and they then can emit even more love.

Each person who is able to throw off their fears and worries and express life with joy will infect all those around them with love and light. It can be easier to write it than to do it sometimes, but it is a choice between being a lesser person than you could be through fear (often of what others will say) or being the person you incarnated to be. Were you born to keep your head down and just get by, or can you find something that makes your heart sing with joy? That's what we mean by not hiding your light under a bushel.

As angels we would like to see every human being filled with joy, love and light. A planet full of happy people is a very different place from a planet of worried and sad people. You could live on a happy planet or a sad one, but the only changes you can really make are in your own lives and hearts.

We mentioned in an earlier book that it is difficult for the Earth as a being of light to have a mass of unhappy people living on her surface creating all that dark energy. She shines like the sun beneath her surface, and you know the sun burns away darkness. You will have the help of the Earth itself in living your lives in light, and by aligning yourself with her it will become easier for you. For this reason we urge you to take advantage of the opportunities she presents to you beginning in 2013 to live happier lives. It may involve some activity on your part, and you will feel the pressure to make changes. There is a push from the prevailing energy now and it will continue to grow from the Earth itself from 2013 onwards. Some activities will atrophy as people don't want to waste their time pursuing them any longer. The activities that lead nowhere or to a dead end will differ from person to person, and you will move away from them. It won't need to take a long time for this change to happen.

We see you as a species milling about aimlessly as each person pursues an individual path. This is a relatively ineffective way to live compared to people joining together in common cause as in politics, trade unions, religions, etc. When you see their example you realise what people can do when working together. Those who join in shared interests and companionship are immediately stronger and learn what it is to be greater than a single individual. At the moment we see your major groups, and political parties are a good example, as a way of dividing humanity. There is too large an element of personal power within the group for it to be a way to learn to love others. Many outside these groups are repelled by this. Political parties are very effective at combining like-minded people while dividing them from others. We would like to see many smaller groups working for the highest good of all and remembering they are all one. When you see a flock of birds you are not thinking about their love for each other, you just see birds flying. Their co-operation and kindness to each other in flight is a good model for you.

The type of small groups we have in mind as good starting places in 2013 are all those where you share your interests with others. A chess club keeps the brain sharp and provides companionship. The Reiki Association in the UK is a group of people from around the country who meet one another at large events, but there are also many small, local sharing groups for those who are interested in practicing Reiki. These can meet once a week or once a month. The important thing is that by meeting together they feel the support of others who share their interests. During those get-togethers they can talk about their experiences when playing chess or practising Reiki. It doesn't matter that everyone does not participate in these particular groups because they are following their own interests. We have an overview of what is happening in your lives and we can see that isolation is a dead end, and getting together is energetically beneficial.

Start a group with an activity close to your heart and invite your friends, and ask them to bring guests. Make new friends doing something you love and let the light shine out in 2013. This will take a little organising, but it will pay you back by taking a small step towards being happy. We are particularly interested in all activities that heal one another or the planet, because that is when you draw even more light through your bodies from the universe. This is also the energy of 2013 and the New Earth, and working with the prevailing energy is easier than working against it. Many of you are healers in different disciplines, and all of these groups will thrive in the future. If we could get all trained healers to meet regularly and channel through light together we would see the levels of light increase on Earth. You can't organise everyone else on the planet, but is there a group you could join or start?

We want to talk about Earth healing groups now and their effect on the planet. When you generously give your time to healing the planet you provide a circle of light that is far bigger than the circle you form physically. The Earth is able to be nourished with light from the universe at these gatherings, in exactly the right vibration for her to use. Those who participate are filled with light by taking part, and you never work alone as we are always there helping you to expand the circle. It's exactly the type of activity closest to our hearts, you are bringing energy and light to the Earth in partnership with humanity, or in other words it makes a difference that you are the ones drawing the energy through your bodies. It is focused, and it has a human imprint because you are Earthly alchemists and have changed the energy by passing it through your bodies and on to the Earth. Bonds are created between people and it gives shared interests a healthy boost, and everyone goes home topped up with healing energy, while we enjoy working alongside you.

Other than these Earth healing evenings we would like to see more outdoor activities where you actually have your feet on the surface of the planet. The less time you spend outside the harder it is to connect to her, and the more time you spend away from her in cities the harder it also becomes. She is covered by human buildings and roads, and it is more difficult for you to feel your connection to her. When you put a man-made obstacle in between you and the Earth you make it harder for yourselves. She is shining as bright as ever, but your own buildings make it more difficult for you to see this. If you look at every other species present on Earth, you are the only ones who built buildings and paved over her. Imagine living at the top of one apartment block and working in another, walking solely on pavements situated above underground tunnels and cables. The Earth is there but you are further removed from feeling her influence.

Perhaps you feel that this is how your life is and it is hard to change it all now, but you could start with small changes such as visits to parks where you actually walk and sit on the ground. You can stand directly on her soil which carries her life within it, even if there are tunnels far underneath. On your annual holidays and vacations you can get out of the cities and for many years people made a real point of doing that; the cultural city-break is relatively new. You may think that animals are living separate lives from you, but many of them remember human/animal interaction through their higher consciousness and they miss people. They know that to join you one day you will have to recognise them for what they are, just as much a small part of the Creator as you are. Today you have pets living with you in your homes and many of you have no other contact with the rest of the animal kingdom. A good rule to remember regarding animals is to treat them the way you would like to be treated yourself, and respect them.

Should you be eating animals? Animals eat other animals and you can eat them too. What we don't like is the way the animals are treated and raised prior to slaughter, and that a great deal of the Earth's surface has been altered to grow food for animals themselves so that you can eat lots of meat. You have become accustomed to high meat consumption and your bodies would be healthier with a smaller ratio of meat to vegetables and fruit. This is advance warning: the new Earth will support actions for the highest good of all, and eating so much meat to make yourselves and the planet sick will cease to work for you.

What do we mean by the Earth supporting the actions that lead to the highest good of all, and who is 'all'? First, you are a tiny part of all, so all is the entire contents of this universe. Your actions will be taken for your own good, and that will mean that an action is holding light for you. That light increases the overall light of your area and that vibration will spread up, down and sideways. It affects your neighbours on Earth and the neighbouring part of your galaxy by raising the quotient of light overall. As the amount of light rises it has a knock-on affect further away, even if it is only like adding a drop of water to a bucket. One day the bucket will be full.

The Earth is a being of light and she shines like the Sun, although she has long provided a familiar and stable surface for you to live on. Her light shines upwards and pressures her guests to end actions that are out of alignment with light. 2012 put pressure on people who found they had to move house, move jobs, and dissolve marriages. Humanity was being squeezed into action. It became impossible to live in an unhappy situation any longer and various strands of their lives came together to give them a big push forwards. The more rubbish that had been swept under the carpet, the more there was to uncover and sort out at that time. For some people it was a step too far and they gave up and refused to move forward.

There was a split in humanity that came about when some had their eyes fixed firmly on the coming light and naturally and smoothly moved into new circumstances; others did not want to see any change and kept their lives exactly the same in every way. What they couldn't imagine was that the energy that supported them in their lives could be withdrawn from them. They would now live out their lives on their own energy alone, having never credited the Earth with any support while they lived here. Their choice was to live on the old Earth with all its ways and ignore the new Earth. They became irrelevant to the future of the planet and mankind.

The people who chose to go forward were overwhelmingly young people. There are older people as well, but the percentage is heavily weighted towards the young. 2012 was governed by older people who owned almost everything and controlled the planet's wealth. While the energy withdraws from them they have a period of exerting control out of old habit but there is no strength left in their voices or bodies. They use their own life force to keep upright and have less energy available for their power plays. Meanwhile young people feel free to make alternate choices for themselves. Very few of them feel the need to work such long hours in grey boxes exerting their control over others. This generation are happier to spend time outside and live lives with a variety of activities in them, and they will be the parents of the next generations.

We talk about generational changes and the years that may pass before large changes take place. This is due to the uncertainty of timings based on a variety of possible human actions. Nothing is set in stone at this point. Change that aligns with light will be very different from what has happened previously in your long history. You would be right in thinking that this happens every 26,000 years, but each time it takes place it's different, and there are always some new players on the planet. They have unique qualities and the combined energy of all the beings alive here is tangible to we who live off-planet. You have assembled on this planet to ascend together, and you are using the increase in light to learn how to ascend and what level of love is needed to fuel the ascension.

Society Turns Upside Down
2013 to 2015

2

Evolution for Humanity

WHENEVER the Galactic timer signals the end of a 26,000 year cycle the Earth remakes herself in the form most useful to her guests. You also have the ability to remake yourselves when you wish by being born again as a baby, or by simply changing your lives. On the 20th of December at 18.20 GMT the old Earth ceased to be, and the new Earth came into being. The only energy present was that of new life and growth, and light was coming from the inside of the planet. Earth is radiating sparkling light straight up out of her surface.

She has also altered the way she feels. In the last cycle Earth felt insubstantial, but this time she has more steeliness and determination. There is only so far you will be able to push her before she pushes back. The Earth's main vibration feels to us primarily like love, but with a strong streak of 'tough love' that is built into her new persona. Earth is the one in control this time around.

This is similar to you playing the same old game, but on a new playing field. As the months and years roll past, you will notice changes taking place that no one could have predicted, and some of these will be due to the change in energy of the planet you live on. There is also an overall feeling of 'it's time to wrap up these games.' If humanity is unable to end its time on Earth in light the other soul groups here are not going to give up their own ascension plans. If there are thousands of species ready to ascend to light and one who is not, they will ascend; they'll be sorry if you don't make it, but they're going anyway. The mere fact that they ascend will help you ascend from another planet at another time if you miss this chance. The new energy is steelier, and less inclined to put up with any nonsense.

The first important date of 2012 was 12.12.12, when the light from the Central Sun began to shine through. This was the beginning of an influx of light: a breath of love and light from the Creator who used the Central Sun to project love into the universe. This light-bath for the planet began the process of cleaning her of thick sludge, and also worked as a galactic timer to let everyone on the planet know that the 26,000 years were up. You use New Year's Day in much the same manner, as a timer announcing a new year and the end of your yearly journey around the sun.

12.12.12 may have reminded you of the twelve dimensions of life in the universe (something that you once knew and that you will know again) from the Divine (level 12) through to level one. The most accurate way to think of the twelve dimensions is like the numbers on a clock face, and not give more importance to any one number than another. It would not be correct to say that one part of the Creator has greater value or importance than another. The influx of energy on 12.12.12 met the Earth, notified her of the renewal time and set in motion her rebirth. It was as if she had an energetic jump-start with outside energy to help her remake herself. For eight days it was very still while all of nature watched, then the old planet was gone and the new planet was the only one in existence. Think of making a papier mache globe around a balloon, when the balloon is popped and drawn out the only structure left is the papier mache globe. It was the same with the Earth. The local Earth winter solstice was not the timer for the beginning of this event. 12.12.12 followed 11.11.11 as dates pre-arranged to help the planet, and your Earthly dates and times were organised to take advantage of the inherent power in numbers.

The number twelve has a place in your world that few other numbers hold. There are twelve numbers on a clock face, twelve zodiac signs, twelve disciples, twelve months, and twelve hallows of Melchizadek in Atlantis, etc. You live in the first three dimensions of height, width and depth. You also live in all the other dimensions, including the twelfth, but you do not recognise them. Not at the moment, but you will. One day you will be like the others who live among you; the animals and insects that can see all of the dimensions. This is a matter of human choice. When the time is right you will see those dimensions again.

How does the rebirth of the Earth affect you as you live here? You are familiar with the phases of the moon where more and more of the moon waxes to become visible until it begins to wane again. Earth's exposure to the Central Sun increased day by day in 2012 until finally she was the only planet in full light at the centre of the galaxy. After the passage of about two weeks the waning began and she slipped behind another planet who then took its turn in the light. The Earth's light bath took the best part of two years to accomplish, the energy built gradually to a peak, and then just as gradually declined. The full exposure to the Central Sun in December brought about the rebirth of the Earth and those changes began to percolate through to you in 2013.

The Central Sun of the galaxy is a very large and bright star. It works with the angels of light and is our ally, and in the distant past we asked it to hold light for the other stars and planets. Your galaxy didn't come about by accident; we communicate with stars and planets, and the beings that inhabit their forms, and we plan and design. We use gravity, force, numbers and all the physical laws that you have discovered, and more. If we did not design a universe how do you think it would end up? Would you learn as fast and easily in complete chaos? You certainly continue to learn in chaos, but those are quite different lessons.

When solar radiation hits Earth from your Sun mutations may occur. Some of you had similar levels of exposure to this light in December 2012. If you were outside as much as possible for those two peak weeks of December you were in unimpeded light, and if you were out in November and January you were exposed to a good amount of light. Many of you were inside because it was winter in the Northern Hemisphere, and you rarely go outside anyway. Your predilection for living and working indoors in boxes has kept you from your Earth mother. The reason we urge you to be outdoors is that the buildings you live in are not natural; they are human/Earth constructions. These buildings carry human energy and may at times work as shields. Each building will be different and some of them have energy that varies from very little to maximum shields. Nothing blocks incoming energy when you're outdoors.

Mutations are many and varied, from bacteria adapting over their brief lifetimes to brand new abilities for human beings. Comic book heroes do not have abilities impossible for you to reproduce. You currently have noticeable variations in your physical forms, far beyond the colour of your eyes or hair. The energy of light at the end of 2012 was the starting point for some new human characteristics. These will begin to be seen in the coming years as you make changes inside yourselves and begin to have children.

Once the changes begin you will have another challenge: to include everyone in your societies as equals no matter what their ability. Right now some of you view those who have different coloured skin as different from you, but some children are born that have greater differences than mere skin colour. We are talking about the way society today excludes those that are seen as impaired, with physical or mental disabilities. The London Paralympics showed that a physical or mental disability did not hold back those who wanted to take part in sport. It is important to remember that you are all human beings together, and you have an opportunity to live with love instead of contempt or hate.

The new December 2012 mutations range from invisible mental improvements to a very small percentage of enhanced physical abilities. There will be changes in the way the brain is utilised, (The brain is currently fully used, it is a myth that areas are unused.) but at the moment your brain takes turns switching areas on and off. Some sections of your brain will be used simultaneously for the first time. Some abilities may seem straight out of Hollywood such as seeing through solid objects or intuitive telepathy. Seeing through solid objects is done by looking straight through one group of atoms that vibrate at a certain overall speed to another group that vibrates at another speed. Any ability that is aligned with the natural laws of the universe will be possible.

The third eye in the centre of your forehead is an organ (don't look for this in medical books, it's energetic only) that allows you to see or sense more dimensions with your eyes closed than you do with eyes open. You see energy more easily with your third eye and it's tuned to seeing what is really there, and is the way you sense the higher dimensions. Your third eye is ready to be used in day to day life as a way of enhancing the information you collect with your normal senses. We see how some of you are ready to leap ahead and learn everything there is to learn. We can also see others, small and emitting no energy but fear; fear that someone will think they are wrong to see so much. They have a long hard road ahead. Those who have plucked up their courage and found groups of friends interested in the same subjects are already using more of their natural abilities, and these groups will continue to move ahead.

In the first part of this book we urged you to spend your free time with those who shared your interests. It's easiest to try out any new abilities when supported by a group. We are not talking about anything that needs to be kept hidden, but practising how to use new abilities without the fear of what other people will say or do.

Mutations of the kind we're talking about will seem amazing the first time you come across them, but the novelty will soon fade. We are only really mentioning them now because we would like all of you to love and support one another. If a person suddenly develops a new ability they may be frightened; loving and accepting them will help them come to terms with change. Afterwards when someone demonstrates a new ability you will all benefit from the new knowledge. It's not always easy to be the first one to do something new without being afraid.

Mutations are often misunderstood. A mutation in the bacterial world often comes about because of the use of pharmaceutical drugs. A small living organism survives its treatment by a drug, and its progeny also survive by breeding a new strain of drug-resistant bacteria. The difference between bacteria and people is that your soul resides in a complex physical body with many capabilities, and these capabilities are turned on like a switch by solar radiation, moving you forward even faster in the new Earth year. Think about what we said about the changes 26,000 years ago in *And I Saw A New Earth* when humanity relinquished living below the waves and moved to dry land. There were a lot of changes for you to get used to at that time. These mutations will be far fewer and less noticeable than those that took place at that time, and yet you are going to change mentally. This is a time when you begin to let go of some barriers you have put up and remember who you are as a soul group. The greater universe is not unknown to you, but you have forgotten all you ever knew about it.

3

Avebury Stone Circle and Music

THE GREAT stone circle of Avebury is now reconnected to the voice and energy of the universe. It is bringing through information in the form of symbols about everything that is happening on the planets and stars you see above. Avebury also reverses the flow of energy and sends information about Earth back up to the stars; in this way the universe is one organism that shares its knowledge. What would you say if you had a mutation that could see and read those symbols? You might be the person who can read them, or perhaps be the person who applies their content. Do you think that on other planets the populations can't read these symbols? Where do the symbols come from in the first place?

Symbols are universal shorthand for words and thoughts. A symbol will deliver a short message encompassing an idea or fact, and half-symbols act as modifiers for complete symbols. If you meditate on a symbol it can take you deeper into knowledge as you contemplate it. Reiki uses symbols in the second degree courses where practitioners work with them enough to understand the uses and meanings of the symbols. Common Earth symbols include road traffic signs and male/female signs for restrooms.

The universe is a living, breathing organism with a life and consciousness of its own. It is vast and has a different purpose than you do; the pulse of the universe is its breath and it can now be felt through your circle at Avebury. You are part of this universe simply because of your presence here, and your greater participation in it will happen when you are ready. It really is the most beautiful place, and our ancient home. The Earth has been silent for many eons of time while Avebury has been neglected and that has been keenly felt, but now she will take her place again. Her Earthly heart was quiet and her strength was hidden, disguising the true nature of the planet you live on. A recent example of strength was Hurricane Sandy in New York, and there was nothing humanity could do to keep the sea water penned in the ocean. The universe, like a human body, consists of a number of organs that work best when connected as a whole and in good condition. The Earth has not been whole or in a good condition for many years.

Avebury is a higher dimensional conduit to the universe with a village existing in the middle of the stones, a little like having a village inside a cathedral. Avebury has been repaired and is working again, but until the village and roads are gone and the stone circle is empty again the final fine-tuning cannot take place. The circle could only function in the higher dimensions up through 2012. One day the village will no longer be there and the circle will be fully working again.

When the circle resumes its full functions it will hum and we know that there will be people who hear and understand the humming it makes. Sound is part of the universe, and sound and shape go together. Some may hear it as singing, and some will hear the rises and falls of tone as the stone circle spins and brings universal energy through. Are you familiar with synesthesia? It is the ability to use one sense in combination with another sense or senses. Synesthesia occurs in a wide variety of combinations. Some people may see letters, numbers, words or music notes in colours, and when some of these people attend an orchestral concert they see colours as well as hear the notes. One may read a page of black print on white paper, and synesthetes may see each letter or number written with a different colour or personality. A little part of their brain seems to be switched on in advance of yours. This is not a mutation but a heightened ability of the brain. The brain is the same, but the ability to access more parts of it simultaneously will be new. The brain absorbs information and clues to give you a picture of events in 3D. A more comprehensive use of the brain will give you a better picture of your world. You will be going from 3D to 5D, and some of you may easily access more than five dimensions. We don't want you to feel there is a limit to what you will be able to do, because there isn't. Sometimes a species requires a big push to move forward, and you received exactly that in December 2012.

Everything with energy has a sound associated with it. Some sounds are screechy and unpleasant and warn you away. Others are very beautiful and reflect the beauty of the soul within. Avebury is made to catch sound in its higher dimensional form along with information. It was designed to be whole and complete by its makers (not human) and would be incomplete without sound. The music of the spheres is a human reference to a very real part of the universe, a universe of sound as well as sight. One day you will begin to notice it, and then you will never be deaf again. Sound is a form of energy.

Music has been discussed in each of the four books we have written with this channel. All music has the ability to focus and bring your attention to a particular energy, to surround and envelope you. Be sure you are surrounding yourself with music that makes you comfortable. Never judge the music that others chose for themselves as it is a very personal choice. Take part in music that makes your heart sing and leave others to find their own path. If you decide to listen to a completely different kind of music then your needs have changed and you will make the necessary switch. If a young person's music seems unsuitable to you, it may be perfect for them and they will change when the time is right. But be aware of having someone else's music forced on you for long periods of time.

What are the sounds that are caught by Avebury right now? The sounds are the sounds of life, and each individual act has a slight sound from a barely audible wisp to the full orchestral sound created by a tropical forest in the moonlight. You may hear the insects and birds, and miss the sounds the plants produce. Because you do not hear these higher dimensional sounds you are not familiar with them, but that doesn't mean they don't exist. One person who really understood the creative power of music was J.R.R. Tolkien, who wrote about the creation of Middle Earth through music by a choir in Ainulindale in *The Silmarillion*. The way he described it makes it understandable to readers, and it's worth reading for a fictional account of how the Earth could have been created. Tolkien used sound to show the creation process, but the actual process took place with pure energy. In his story sound is the form of energy used to create a planet.

We were for the most part speaking about recorded music earlier, but the real benefits are in taking part by singing and playing your own instruments. There are singers who are vessels for the emotions of music and help their audiences to feel those emotions. Music can carry emotions and make it easier for musicians to touch the hearts of their audiences. Making music is universal, and often brings a smile to the listeners' face. It touches the part of you that existed before time began.

Many people have trouble accessing their emotions, or are only able to access a few of them. Think about this; a whole person has a full range of emotions and to say one is less good than another is untrue. Sometimes fear is exactly the right emotion, it can take you away from a dangerous situation quickly. Some people don't give or receive love. Do you want to imitate them, or do they need some help? Why should any emotion be better than another? Now take a singer who touches your heart with the beauty of the original music and his/her interpretation of how the emotions in the music should be expressed. There are people who may feel the emotion present in the song only when helped by the vibration of the music combined with the sound of the singer or musical instrument. They may be introduced to the emotion by listening to the music, and begin to understand love or sorrow, etc. from that day.

For these reasons we like making music more than listening to music. What you get from listening to music is a pale shadow energetically to that of producing music yourself. Music is important, one of the building blocks of creation in the universe, and you as creators benefit from being involved in music. There are gifted musical healers, talented people who change the vibration of their clients with sound energy. If you are part of a band or choir you will also benefit by being immersed in their sound. It's time now for healing, and changing your energy with music helps you do that.

Music is below your feet inside the Earth. In a universe

of tuneful sound the Earth has its own song. Because many of you don't walk barefoot outside but instead live indoors you don't hear or feel this sound. However there are many people that do live closer to the Earth and they incorporate into their drumming the heartbeat of the Earth. The Earth pulses this beat out into the universe to be heard and felt by the other planets and stars. The sound we hear back from them at Avebury is also vibrational but varies from the deepest steady beat to the flighty tune of a small active body. All sounds have their origin in the universe and its Creator, and deliver a message to the listener. Encoded into the songs that arrive here are all the little flourishes of life bound up together into an overall melody. One person's life could add a trill to a melody, while another's could be a steady beat. It takes all kinds of beings and sounds to make up a universe full of life.

There can be clean beats, and there can be muddy sounds in music making it either sharp or flat. Sometimes there is silence. The Earth was not able to broadcast her sounds to the outer universe until Avebury was repaired in May 2012 and the great three-dimensional ball was set to spin. Walking through Avebury you see a flat, two-dimensional circle, but it is a twelve-dimensional ball with each dimension spinning in a different direction. Spinning in all directions at once keeps the circle stationary on Earth. A little like a gyroscope, it doesn't travel away from it location at Avebury. The old stones you see and touch can be changed and substituted without altering the incoming energy. When people first walked into the energetic circle of Avebury they added some large stone markers so they could find it again. The stones added their own qualities to the circle, and bring through a different energy for each stone, a little like hollow straws. In the past people were healed by locating the stone they wanted to spend some time with, because that stone had a portion of the overall energy coming through that resonated with that person. The circle changed its function and it was now energy with stones and people. What is happening right now is that the circle partially works as it should for healing. The missing stones make it harder for many people to connect with them, but they are still present in the higher dimensions. The higher dimensions are functioning normally, but the lower dimensions need to be supported and repaired.

4

Why is Everything So Difficult?

HUMAN SOCIETY has been built on a series of lies, one lie on top of another like blocks. This means you have all adjusted to a way of living using the rules you understand to stay alive. There's a lot of grumbling that life isn't always fair, but the extent of this unfairness would leave you speechless if you could clearly see the truth. There is almost no truth left in your societies, and you have adjusted to that also. The great majority of people are honest, but most people inadvertently lend their support to those who lie. They have become easy prey for ruthless people who only want to live at the expense or the happiness of others. There are many who lack compassion or have an empty set of morals, and are blind to truth and the pain of living when surrounded by lies. They think nothing of adding one more lie to the sum total. They have not only adapted, but contribute to building the walls higher.

Abraham Lincoln was only a young man when he visited the slave markets in New Orleans. In the 1800's many did not believe slaves had properly developed human feelings and would not care if their spouse or child were sold to another plantation. Lies like these underpinned an unhappy civilisation and caused the deaths of so many men and women in slavery and an ugly civil war. Lincoln waited and gambled everything on an unpopular chance to end slavery in the USA. We often feel sorry that there are very few of you who see your world clearly, but we are grateful for rare people like Lincoln. Look at the situation before Lincoln freed the slaves and after, and how life is lived today many years after slavery ended. Keeping a slave denied the person was a fellow human being.

There are those among you who are sensitive to thoughts, especially lies. In fact almost all of you know when you are being lied to and what do you do? You say nothing because to challenge a lie is worse than to quietly pretend to accept it and walk away. Do you ever listen to lies being told in the various media and wait for someone to challenge them? Challenging consists of the one who is being lied to, who is often on the outside of the situation, *proving* a lie was delivered barefaced into a camera or microphone. It may not be possible to do this very quickly. But sometimes those telling lies rely on not being challenged in public by others as it is considered disrespectful or rude. What is a good way to challenge someone as a liar, or bring the truth back into everyday life? This is about more than one TV interviewer who does not ask for the truth, this is a society-wide problem of how that particular newscaster would be regarded if they asked very challenging questions. These kinds of questions are usually confined to a courtroom, and evidence is provided to back up the charges. This is how hard it is right now to make people responsible for what they say and do. If you think of what people are prepared to say in public, what are they saying behind closed doors?

When we angels called this part of the book 'Society Turns Upside Down' we were looking at the possibility of people turning around this entire situation of living in a world created by lies. You would do this by acknowledging to yourself that you are being lied to, and deciding that you've had enough. You won't be alone, and asking for the truth gets easier each time you do it. And then you will find out that you are in the majority and that most ordinary people are honest.

This is how we see you at the moment: as a vast number of hard-working, kind and loving people who do their best. But we also see you trying to walk forward in your lives up to your knees in syrup, and fighting through thick, sticky spider webs. You deserve better, you deserve a fair chance at living and a clear path forward without obstacles. The whole idea behind the new Earth in 2013 is to change the energy to light, to burn away the syrup and the spider webs so you can move forward on your chosen path in your lives. Everyone could move forward swiftly, but some people are very set in their ways. We hope they'll enjoy the experience of change, but we will not do it for them.

Others, and that includes you if you are reading this, we hope will have made some changes in 2012 so that you are free to move forward as soon as you can in 2013. The energy of light and love squeezes you in the right direction, and this is an individual path for your highest good. Some of you sold your homes as early as 2011 and have been waiting ever since for a change you could feel was going to happen, others are talking about the need to move in 2013. Take the person who sold their house and is ready to go where they will be the most happy, and compare them to someone who is getting ready to move. The main difference is that the first person will be happy at an earlier date. The second person will still be sorting out their old world stuff before they can take off and move forward. Or it is possible they may have too much to do at once and have a slower start. We want everyone to be happy because happiness is light.

The first and most important change in society is to ask others to have the courtesy to tell you the truth. The second is finding what you need to do to make your heart sing with joy. Which task will you find easier?

5

Swap Money for Happiness

HAPPINESS spreads from one person to another, and when you get a group of happy people together their energy spreads further out to others. Imagine a residential street where everyone loves their job, but has enough time at home to enjoy their families and do some gardening. What would that street be like? The neighbours could be smiling because they were home long enough to meet each other and form a community. It could be clean and attractive because people were proud of their community and homes. Most importantly you would be able to get to know your children as individuals and spend time with them, raising them and teaching about life. In societies that function well, this is all a part of life.

How far back in your own country's history did this stop happening? We want to talk about the change in energy that took place in home life. Economically speaking there was a shift from living with what people had, to coveting what people had. There was a change away from providing the basics for health, i.e. food and shelter in warm houses, a way of paying for these, and having time to enjoy yourselves. Once people began to desire nicer vacations (flying instead of travelling by car or train) bigger and bigger houses and more possessions, everything had to change to provide this. People spent their lives making things that could be bought by others, and the economy became based on consuming more and more products. For millennia your economies have been based on making a lot of items that needed to be sold, and sold in greater amounts every year. In this economic model the day people stop buying an ever-increasing amount of goods those factories will close down and those former employees will not have the money to keep buying. This shuts down more factories. But wasn't it always like this?

There was a long period of time when people lived in modest dwellings and once they had acquired the basics to cook, eat and keep warm they bought very few new items. They were content to work for their living as craftsmen or farmers and spend more time at home. They did not need to buy enough goods to fill a large house or employ staff to look after everything they bought. They were respected for their honesty, wisdom and conversation, not the size of their homes or bank accounts. Factories were fewer and the work was more varied. In the past the smith was a skilled person who did a variety of jobs all day long that challenged his abilities. Today cheap metal goods are manufactured on an assembly line, and they break. But what would you rather do, work at a job with variety that challenges you or do one thing on an assembly line? (There will also be a place for assembly lines and people who enjoy working on them, but not as many as there are now.)

You cannot have rising consumption without an ever-increasing population around the world. Yet you know that there are so many humans already on Earth that the other species have been pushed to the margins of the available land on the planet. This is not right. To accept a level population or a declining one will mean less consumption of goods and less employment making new items to sell. Factories and production of goods will decrease with a shrinking population, and everyone will chase overseas markets hoping to sell abroad. You used to have an alternate economic model where you made do with less, and you relied on a stable population and support from the planet. There will be recycling from one home to another, and you will not need to work so hard because you will not spend so much. This is a recipe for social change through economics, and it will happen. For you to come through this easily is to let go of your excess possessions and beliefs, enjoy the company of other people, and live closer to your places of work.

There could be no larger change for you than to switch to a new economic reality from the current one of ever-increasing consumption tied to an increasing birth rate. One previous economic reality was cities surrounded by farmland without high population growth. Families were smaller everywhere and goods were more durable. Already you may wonder how everyone made a living when they were not producing and selling goods all day long. They only produced as many goods as they could sell, and they had the rest of the day off to do other things. They grew and picked food, went out in the evenings with friends, went for walks, and raised their children. Their homes were only as large as they needed to be and did not take a lot of maintenance. The important thing was that shopping was not recreational and the foundation of all economic growth in society. It was pleasurable but people bought less to put in their smaller homes. Actually, they were not in their homes so much because they were outside. They were in contact with the Earth, and that kept them sane and happy. It was a society where people knew each other, and they kept an eye on everyone that lived nearby. You do not need to be afraid to change to this kind of an economic and social model.

There is a choice being offered to you right now, to relax your grip on your bank accounts and trust that the future will be fine, or to hang on tight. The whole flow of energy in the universe means exactly that - flow. Something goes out, and it makes space for something else to come in. Hanging onto your possessions is choking off flow, so nothing can come in. It's ok to spend money because you are always being looked after, and there is always movement and flow. What is not ok on a personal level is to stop spending any money, and to stop trusting that you will always be alright. We do not mean looked after by the state with welfare or benefits. We are talking about the energy of receiving, the softness that allows something to come into your personal energy fields. The thoughts of trust and love that create softness in your hearts are the same thoughts that allow good things to come to you. The fearful thoughts that scream lack and emptiness draw lack and emptiness to you. Good things literally bounce off your hard exterior and go elsewhere.

There will be more time for love and friendship, and less time spent earning money. We know that some of you are very good at attracting money, and others are very good at attracting love into their lives. We want the two to balance, so that the very successful also get to spend time with their families, and for families to have enough money to make ends meet. The least amount of happiness we've ever seen has stemmed from what some of you call the "rat race". You are working far too hard to accumulate objects that do not by themselves confer happiness. You use possessions to show others how well you have done in your lives and how successful you are.

Again, we are looking at the type of energy you as a species are broadcasting. We see many different ways of being unhappy. What do you need in your lives to be happy? Can you be happy if you are respected for something other than the size of your home or your bank accounts? Just going by what we have observed in your long history, you were happier in earlier times.

Houses are shelter and when you are surrounded by children you need a bigger home, and people without children need smaller ones. Home owning has become stagnant. If you go with the flow of energy in your lives you will not resist moving home at the right time. The energy around homes is only part of the stagnant energy of possessions, but as the largest possession on the planet it will certainly affect the overall energy of riches and poverty. Ancient Rome had marble palaces for the few and slaves to look after them. You have recreated those palaces now with your few rich people owning home after home with housekeepers and servants looking after the empty properties.

Some people have become rich with your help; you bought the goods they made and you support them in their lifestyles. You buy something new these days when the old one breaks. You could repair or give old items away, except repairs are now more difficult to come by. The economy will go into freefall and change will happen because of this imbalance. Large employers will disappear and there will be new, smaller ones hiring people and these businesses could be closer to your home. Men and women will each take care of the children while working shorter hours and still have enough to eat and stay warm. If everything was turned upside down and you were happier as a result, can you hold onto that thought and keep going? After a few years of chaos life would follow a new path for most of you. We said earlier you could learn different lessons from chaos.

Some of you have been looking forward to a wonderful life on the new Earth. We can see a vast reservoir of unhappiness, and it will take a correction to get back on track. Your economy is based on a flawed model and it will crash sooner or later. The energy of the new Earth will pour light into this system and the light will help you make the necessary changes. At the same time there will be satisfying work for many of you who currently work terribly hard at jobs just to earn a living. Small businesses will begin to thrive and they will be supported by the energy; perhaps you will start your own business.

It can be terrifying to enter a period of rapid change, but it doesn't have to be a bad experience. As with so many other things this is a matter of how you perceive the changes. In the case of international economics it was a broken system and did not work well except for a very few wealthy people. You were never going to have as much money as they do; everything was skewed in their favour. Everyone should have the chance to be with their children as they grow up, and spend time with their families.

It is a complete turnaround to change from a society that is consumption-based into a society that is balanced and happy. You will be giving up that feeling of never having enough to one of relaxed, stress-free peacefulness. There will be a lot of poor economic news in the next few years, but there already is in many parts of the world. There seems to be unsolvable problems in the eurozone. Even in a big country like China that relied on the West to buy everything their factories could manufacture, production slowed down when people stopped buying. What you can do in your own lives is to accept this, and look for the energy to support smaller businesses. If you were in a smaller business that was going from strength to strength, and had enough money to buy food and shelter, entertain friends and go out, could you let go of being unhappy? It's a swap: money for happiness.

You may think this is very simplistic, but we look at your stressful lives and the unhappy vibrations you emit and are relieved that you received the help of the 2012 energy. The system you have been part of is unhealthy, and the 2012 energy was also about health. Some of you already have enough of everything and many others do not. Your world has gone as far as it can go in the direction of consumption.

How fast can economic change take place? Are we really saying that there will be an end to inequality and a new way of living together? Right now the markets are set up to sell, sell, sell. What happens if people feel they just don't have the money to buy? They won't buy goods and services and those that were manufactured will be left behind on the shelves. In the past there have been reforms that patched together the economic systems and kept them going in the same direction as before. What is different this time is the new energy, the energy of light and healing. It is going to support actions that unite people and allow them to move forward towards the light. Inequality does not unite people, it drives them further apart. The steps that you take to move forward towards light will unite people and show love. It is time to remember that you are one soul, and treat others as an extension of yourself. This cannot co-exist with inequality and treating others as if they are not as good as you. With great wealth comes arrogance, and arrogance sees others as inferior. From time to time a wealthy man says that he cares deeply for everyone, but we only ask that you watch his actions, not listen to his words.

To protect yourselves and your families look to the future we have outlined. How do you fit into that scenario? Can you look forward with joy to changes that will make you happy? Will you be able to let go of excess possessions and move into a smaller home that requires less heat and light? The more you are able to let go effortlessly, the easier it is to move forward.

We keep saying you will all want to move forward and the energy of the new Earth will support your lives. Anything not supported by energy loses strength and becomes hollow and brittle. You may have changed your life completely so that you are already happy, perhaps you previously let go of old thought patterns and possessions and moved ahead. That has happened with some people, and they used the energy to lever themselves out of stagnant positions. Now the new Earth is actually here and the push must feel overwhelming to some of you; to move to a career you would love to do, or a new place to live. Once you take those steps you will be carried forward by the flow of energy and it will make it easier to pursue a happy life. Remember, we measure success by happiness, not by money. Money is a human invention.

We angels do not carry money on us, nor do we provide money if you should ask us for it. We look at money and we see a river of energy, the energy of exchange overlaid with the energy of corruption. Money is a convenient way to run an economy and exchange your goods and services. It is a step up from bartering, which was very limiting and inflexible compared to cash. At the bottom of the river of energy is this pure use of money, but it is overlaid with greed as it became easy for some to help themselves. Sometimes these takings are earned and just, and sometimes they are excessive. After a while, by 2012, it was as if the river of energy was lined by people taking out as much cash as they could with two hands, and it began to falter and run dry for lack of flow. People did not benefit from continuing to use money in the way it had always been used, as a medium of exchange.

Money has no intrinsic value as a piece of paper, only the value you give to it, and how much you can buy with it. This is important, that a plain piece of paper buys nothing but the printed money buys goods for you. It is solely a creation of human beings and you must support it with your own energy. There is your clue as to how easy it is to walk away from money towards all the things that have genuine value. Your monetary system is only as strong as you make it, and if you walk away and stop shopping it will collapse. It is very fragile.

Built over the river of money were the grand buildings that are home to banks. They make good profits handling money, and they were just one of the players taking money from those who worked hard to earn a living. Banks are a part of a larger system that allows them to exist in their present forms. Whatever has happened with banks is a symptom of a greater imbalance. We see the energy, we see the factors that impede the flow of money, we see the leakages into private accounts, and we see how money is used. We can see it because it is energy and flow.

The majority of people who supported money with their own energy were supported by the Earth. A small percentage of these people moved forward with the new Earth, and a large majority of people were left supporting money with their own energy, at a time when the old Earth they stood on was gone. The new Earth is where the energy is, and it is the only planet that now exists. How long can the monetary systems last when the energy is withdrawn? You're about to find out. One piece of advice is to put your own money somewhere safe where you will not worry about it. Worry is not a useful activity. There is a role for banks in any society that needs to borrow money for a new house or a new business. Banks do not need to vanish, but your banks have the risky energy of a casino at the moment, and they are top-heavy with salaries and bonuses which makes them less stable. The most important thing to remember here is that the new Earth will not support any activity that is not for the highest good of all.

Expand this scenario into all of the large corporations in existence. A few people are going forward into the new Earth and will continue their business. A great many others will struggle without Earth energy and fail. Many of you will only realise what this energy does for you when it is gone from your lives.

When the economies of the most affluent nations run into difficulties, the people living inside those countries will also struggle to find enough money. A new economy will emerge, one that is not based on consumption of goods, but one where people are happy with the things they own. They will buy less, and work less, and a large adjustment will have to be made to take account of this.

We can see vibrant people making happy lives for themselves doing things they love. They do not miss supporting governments, giant corporations or large wealthy organisations. They are happy to buy something from a neighbour and save themselves time and travel. Smaller, energy-efficient homes do not require as many objects to fill them. Priorities will change and governments relying on sales tax for income will find the amount decreases as less is spent on goods and services. These changes will take place at different speeds. There are people who chose to move forward with the new Earth, and there are those who will never notice any change took place at all.

Predicting economic growth in terms of consumption will give the wrong information and introduce lower revenues for governments when their tax income decreases. The ideal tax rate is the one where everyone voluntarily pays an amount to achieve the services that are really needed like schools, roads and hospitals. An imbalance has occurred in your tax and expenditure, and it is possible to rebalance it. The new Earth supports balance.

Expected Changes in Food Production 2013 to 2018

6

Plants Have Energy Bodies Too

THE WAY humanity feeds itself will begin to correct itself between the years 2013 to 2018. Because you have distanced yourselves from food production and cooking you barely receive enough energy from food to keep you healthy. It's popular to say that eating well is boring or unimportant to your health, and yet increasing rates of disease and infertility are reported and the connection between eating well and health is not sensibly discussed. Researchers visit the farms of the healthy-eating Mennonites in Minnesota just to discover how they are able to maintain a fertility rate near 100%.

In a planet as lush and teaming with life as the Earth something has happened to the food people eat: it is degraded of health-giving nutrients and devoid of natural energy. Filling your stomachs with just any food does not mean that you are eating to maintain your health. It matters what you eat, the variety you eat, and whether the food is fresh or not. The energy available in food contributes to your own health and energy. You need to eat something that is alive to maintain your own life force. One harvested, the energy in plants slowly diminishes over time.

A number of studies have been done with people eating raw food, cooked food, or junk food but we want to talk about food as it comes out of the fields. The energy of the crops has diminished and some of the cooking methods further reduce the available energy. In your societies cooking is dividing into those who never cook and either eat out or put a ready-made meal in the oven and increasingly fewer home cooks. There is more distance now between the person and the food being eaten, and in that distance there is loss of energy. You see something similar in the way electricity is lost when it travels down the wires away from a power station.

The next five years will see some of the current agricultural methods of production reversed as smaller farms grow a wider variety of crops and animal husbandry becomes more widespread. New people will become farmers but they will not want to go down the established farming routes of today. Some people will enter into farming by accident as they look for a way to feed themselves and discover that they want to increase their animal stock or grow more crops. Food won't travel as far before it's eaten, and will be eaten in a fresher state.

7

Farming Changes

MANY CHANGES have taken place in farming methods since the 1940s and the Second World War. Change was never intended to happen this way, but as food production was mechanised and yields improved there was a decrease in the energy native to the crops. Each plant is an energetic being in a physical body and the heavy application of all-purpose fertiliser disregards some of the natural requirements of the plant. Prior to World War II farms were smaller and life could be very difficult for the farmer. Why would anyone devote themselves to running such a risky business, at the mercy of the weather and insects? But surprisingly, people who worked outside at a variety of jobs all day long, as farmers did, were often content. Many farmers on good land have become prosperous and respected in their communities. Farming is different all around the world, and food is the one of the requirements (with clean air and water) for life. From the fertile soil of the river valleys to the terraced fields of the mountain regions, food crops have been grown for millennia.

A few hundred years ago a farmer would sell to a middleman or wholesaler, who then found buyers for the food, whether in the market, a hotel or restaurant. Today this system has become top heavy, where the middlemen and the supermarkets often dictate to the farmer his profit level on the crops grown to their exacting standards. Food that grows naturally is often an irregular shape, but you would never know this when shopping in the supermarkets today.

When a wholesaler purchases a crop he ships it to the next buyer; it could be a large bread factory or a supermarket. With centralisation there are a lot of food miles shipping almost everything you eat. Food is flown around the world to be eaten out of season and countries themselves are becoming increasingly specialised. Crops are grown in poor countries that locals never get the chance to taste, such as green beans in Kenya. When food is shipped for miles and miles the consumer pays, and the pollution decreases the vitality of the air. No one wants to live next to a busy road full of trucks taking food to a central depot, yet food is taken miles to warehouses before being shipped out again and sold. Your method of putting food on the table has dirtied the air you breathe, and contributed to the Earth being drained of oil. In your own lives you do not waste fuel as you clearly see the fuel gauge going down when you run your cars. But you are paying for the fuel used by these large transport firms when you buy groceries.

You have always needed air, food and water living here on Earth. Once it was a gift to you; if you ate the freely available food you would not have to find another way of producing energy to maintain life. It is possible to live here without food, but it takes insight and dedication to learn how to live on pure energy, and most people die of old age before they ever learn how. The Earth agreed to be bountiful, to provide the necessary requirements for growing food easily. It provided sun and rain in balance, and could raise a crop from nothing to fully grown overnight. Food was never meant to be a problem for humanity because it is a necessity and you can't live without it. It has become highly profitable for some, because people keep coming back over and over again to buy more. It's not addictive, but it has the same selling pattern as an addictive substance. It is one of the largest global industries these days, with an organised structure that provides fresh food in shops around the world. Is there any reason to wish for this to change?

We angels never eat, why would we? We are pure energy and prefer to sun ourselves in the light of a nearby star, but we care for all living things including the plants and animals you eat. We can see sick fields of crops that appear healthy until you look at the energy they give off, and then we watch that very same food being eaten by you. You are trying to maintain healthy bodies on a diet of unhealthy food, grown without the necessary nutrients that the crop developed with over time. In the last seventy years you have laced your fields with pesticides and fertilisers and the average field of cereal crops is reeling energetically from this. The fact that these crops grow at all is a miracle. (Here is an example of love in unexpected places, a field of grain doing its best to provide a crop out of love for those who will one day eat it.)

The application of chemical fertilisers to a field means that only those three nutrients (NPK – nitrogen, phosphorus, and potassium) are present in the crop. They are good for making the crop grow and appear healthy. The human body requires far more nutrients than NPK fertiliser formulated for plant growth. Where are you going to get the other nutrients necessary for life? By eating even more vegetables and fruits that were grown with the same three nutrients? There is a problem here with the government regulation of fertilisers. In Finland they legislated to add selenium to the mix, which had the end result of fewer heart attacks and less cancer in the overall population. That was by adding one missing nutrient. You can't have selenium in the crops unless it's in the soil first, and if it's not in the soil it could be part of the fertiliser mix, if you had human health as a goal instead of plant yields.

Before the advent of chemical fertilisers, animal manure and seaweed were used to add nutrients to the fields. In an island nation like Great Britain the seaweed was dragged up onto the fields to decompose over the winter. The heavy rains on the island caused the nutrients to wash out of the soil during the year and into the water and the seaweed used these nutrients to grow strong. At the end of the season the farmer used the seaweed to restore the soil. This cycle kept the fields fertile, and when manure was used the nutrients eaten by farm animals were returned to the soil after being broken down by the animal's digestive track. Plants use cellulose to form rigid cell walls to stand upright and cooking or grinding with teeth releases the nutrients from the cell's interior. This is why cooking food like carrots can be a good idea. Seaweed and manure contain cellulose from plants and are also soil conditioners in that they keep the soil from becoming too compacted.

World War II changed the landscape of the farm in Great Britain by removing the farm animals to make way for cereal crops like wheat. Bread was always available during rationing in Britain, but meat was tightly controlled. After years of war and growing grain over and over again on the same fields there was insufficient manure on the farm to feed the crops and yields began to decline. The large chemical companies provided NPK to be spread on the fields and the crops grew lush once again. The vast numbers of plough horses from the 1930's were slaughtered and replaced by tractors, and the vets and blacksmiths that looked after the horses declined in numbers. The life in the countryside was almost unrecognisable to the returning soldiers.

What is farming like today in many first world countries? The giant tractors protect the farmer in his air-conditioned cab while the ploughed rows are guided by a satellite for straightness. The moisture content of the soil is provided on a computer printout, again read by satellite. The living plants have less contact with the farmer, and they have become objects rather than fellow life forms. There was a time when a farmer could tell the moisture content of a field from a wealth of previous experience. This is in danger of being lost as a skill passed down from farmer to farmer. Do you need to go back to horse-drawn ploughs and no satellites? It depends on how high the tractor diesel prices rise in the future, and whether the satellite charges are affordable, or even available. These farmers are grain farmers, and that was once unheard of, to put all your risk into one crop. The diversification of farming was a safety net against poor crop yields. Even in the Great Depression of the 1930's there were often eggs to sell and poultry manure for the farm. As a species you are backing yourselves into a corner of technology with regards to your food supply, you are putting all your eggs in one basket. In farming the ability to pass on knowledge to the next generation was priceless.

Farmers are always busy; it is a day-long job that is not 9 to 5. They live at work, are on call every hour of the day, and grow food so the rest of you have something to eat. Most of them would not change places with you for another kind of life. So what's so great about farming? Farmers are their own boss and choose how to spend their days; they are outside and physically active and have variety in their working lives. These ingredients go toward making a happy life, although there are some farmers on marginal land where it is difficult to farm prosperously. Farmers also can grow fresh food and are well-fed from their own vegetable gardens in the summer. Why buy food when you can grow it? If you eat fresh food you will be taking in all the nutrients of that plant and do not have to use any of your own vitality to absorb it. Plants slowly lose their life-force over time when in storage. Kinesiologists can check the level of life force present in food with muscle testing and see the before-and-after results for many different methods of cooking.

There is a way to remove the life force from food entirely, and that is by using a microwave oven. Kinesiologists can tell you that fresh food that is cooked in a microwave will go in at a level of ten out of ten, and come out at zero. The food cooked in these ovens saps the vitality of the people that use them most frequently. We see the energy, and of all the side effects from microwaving food, this is the most serious to us. You are all beings of energy and you maintain your health by taking in the energy of food. We realise that very few people detect energy at the moment, but there are many on the planet right now that could do so if they began to look for it. Microwaves negate the main reason you take in food, which is to increase your own energy and live a full life. Cooking food in the traditional way of applying heat in an oven, steaming or boiling, etc. will affect the energy levels remaining in the food, but not by very much. A six month old potato that has become rubbery has more energy than microwaved food and it will still send up green shoots.

Twenty years ago in Chengdu in China (and other places

around the world) local food markets provided live animals and fresh vegetables that were bicycled into the city centre daily. The food was fresh or it wouldn't sell, and the smaller animals were killed at home. It sounds gruesome, but there was no distance between the family and the food being eaten, and it was a normal part of life. The loss of energy in the food was the least it could be short of eating a live animal, which people choose not to do. The distance between the consumer and the food is far, far greater now with factories producing most food and shipping it. The food is not fresh; it is days old and it's made from the cheapest ingredients that can be sourced. The combination of ingredients is only acceptable if you keep yourself ignorant of what you're eating. China has swung from a society that ate healthily with fresh food and a high vegetable to meat ratio, to one that is adopting a Western fast food diet.

The fact that the Western diet is high in fat, sugar and salt is well known, but the downside includes early death and living with poor health. Fat, sugar and salt are cheap ingredients, and are eaten in far greater quantities than at any other time in human history and they affect the health of the body. Those who rely on take-away meals are eating a meal heavy in fat and salt, and their children do not learn to cook or eat healthily. People fill their bodies with substances that decrease the quality of their lives. We look at this and grieve; we know that you have been manipulated, and that your weaknesses have been exploited to make money for others. The combination of chemicals attached to your foods can have addictive qualities, such as the neuroexcitatory flavourings attached to potato crisps or chips. The only way for you to avoid being manipulated by your food is to buy fresh ingredients and prepare them at home. For some this advice comes too late as they no longer know how to prepare a meal from fresh ingredients.

There is a failure in the West in understanding the role of food in personal health. Preparing meals is simply not done in some homes, and all meals are purchased. The children never learn to cook and cannot feed themselves unless they buy food. Some people come home, shove a ready-made meal in the oven and watch TV or use the computer while it cooks. They have run out of time and the first cut is to food preparation, and a lecture on fresh food falls on deaf ears. This makes us very sad.

Do you want to be vibrantly healthy? The energy levels of the food you eat are a big part of health. Fertilisers from a lab are energetically inert, while the same chemicals found in nature have the energy belonging to the Earth. When you apply NPK from a lab you are not increasing the energy levels of the crop. A diamond made in the lab has no energy and does not compare to a real diamond from a mine. The same price cannot be charged for man-made diamonds. Health comes from a number of different ingredients, and one of them is the energetic value of your food and drink. Do you microwave all of your hot drinks? You lose the energy native to water and are drinking something lifeless. Alcohol has a low vibration, and you can stand in the alcohol aisle of a store and feel how different it is to your own energy. Alcohol is an acquired taste that is not recommended for children, as it could poison them. Adults learn to cope with the energy and the taste. This is not necessarily detrimental unless it is drunk regularly or to excess when it can kill people. Alcohol is a depressant – it decreases your levels of happiness over time.

In addition to the lack of natural energy, farming with chemical fertilisers and pesticides is very expensive. Another trial you could make is to stand in the chemical aisle of a garden centre and feel the vibrations of the weed killers and pesticides. Then quickly move on. There is a small movement in farming in the USA where the money is not spent on chemicals but instead is used to hire a number of men to work on the farm manually in the traditional way and feed and house their families. When these families move into a town the schools begin to fill, the local shops and stores are patronised and it becomes livelier. It's been generations since the drift to the cities began, but it could be reversed. If all the farms around former farm towns were full of hired men that lived locally with their families, these towns would be rejuvenated. Everyone has paid a very high price for the use of chemicals, not just the farmer who bought them.

Chemicals in farming are often seen as an easy way out. They have helped to fuel a green revolution of high yields and helped the farmer to produce a crop in spite of pests and poor soil. Farmers themselves are handling these products before applying them, and these carry low vibrations, far lower than those of the person handling the bags. When you vibrate at one level, and spend time with something of a vastly reduced level of energy you are working hard to maintain your own health. Using chemicals with a low level of energy, or no energy, affects the health of the crop and the health of the person who eats the food.

Food vibrations are very interesting, and no two plants or animals are the same. For example, alcohol expands your energy fields and helps the mood at a party, while salt contracts these same energy fields and salty snacks brings you back into balance. Plants naturally grow where the vibration of the planet supports their growth, and people eat a multitude of plants. By growing large fields of one crop you are ignoring the planet underneath, and reducing the variety of foods you eat.

Chemicals not only lack energy and are inert when added to food, but you are not able to make use of them in your bodies as you do with organic food. Some pass through with little harm, some replace natural foods and others interfere with the body. Do you really want to eat something that has the potential to make you ill? Everything added to a foodstuff is put there for the benefit of the producers and sellers of the food. The chemicals allow them to decrease spoilage and wastage until it is off their hands and you have bought it from them. Preservatives are not needed in fresh foods. The effect on your bodies of a large number of preservatives is to clog you up, physically and energetically. In our view everything is energy and it's either flowing or stagnant. The human body is healthiest when there is movement in all systems, and least healthy when it is stagnant. First the body's energy is stagnant, and then the body itself is stagnant. We know we said that chemicals lack energy, but preservatives act as energy black holes, sucking your own good energy into them and holding it where you can't access it. The more preservatives you eat the less energy you have left. What does this do to you? It takes away the vibrancy of your life and you end up tired or unwell at a younger age.

But farming is hard, isn't it? That was the old planet Earth with a different feel about it. This is a new planet and she wants to move forward with you, not opposed to you. As you walk outside now you can feel life through your feet, and there is a sparkle in the air, and that is the Earth to speak to and work with. She's not far away and she's listening. Every time you consciously draw her energy up through your feet you change yourself with her help.

There are people now alive who want to move forward, and there are people who don't want to do this at all. It won't always be this way, that there are two kinds of people on one planet. The best advice is to go forward yourself, make your own life in the direction you want to go, and don't worry about the others. You needn't carry any one else along with you.

8

Chemicals in Water

YOUR WATER, which you need to live, is so contaminated now with chemicals that some people are made ill by it. The amount of prescribed anti-depressants entering the water supply in the north of England through urination is measurable. They are present in every glass of water there and are also part of the ingredients of any food or drink (such as beer) that calls for water. The population's ability to engage with life is reduced by anti-depressants.

The female hormone estrogen/oestrogen is part of the reproductive pill, but it is also an easily adaptable molecule that is used in the manufacture of plastic water bottles and can form one of the bases for making crop fertilisers. Your water around the world is contaminated with the female hormone oestrogen, and men and women drink it. The xenoestrogens in the water are produced in the laboratory for these products and are different from natural oestrogens (they must be or they cannot be patented) and they behave differently in the body. They have an affinity for breast tissue and once attached to a cell that is waiting for a natural oestrogen molecule to arrive and stimulate it, will sit on these cells and stimulate them non-stop. They are very difficult to dislodge. Natural oestrogen will stimulate a cell and move out of the body, giving the cell a rest period. Natural oestrogens are found in vegetables. The effect on the breast of being stimulated non-stop is suspected to be a cause of serious illness.

The presence of oestrogen in your water and plastic water bottles makes it hard for you to avoid. It is not removed by a charcoal filter, and you must drink water to live. This is a case of dirtying your own nest. You may reduce the amount of oestrogen consumed by buying water in glass bottles, and some people have seen their pear-shaped hips reduce as their oestrogen levels reduce. You are used to seeing teenage girls with large breasts now, but girls used to be fully mature before growing so large. Men are dealing with levels of oestrogen in their bodies they've never had to cope with before.

Oestrogen is only one of the many, many chemicals that you ingest daily. It is no coincidence that the most polluted parts of the world have the highest levels of disease and infertility. The Earth has areas now that are fairly toxic and some people have made a great deal of money poisoning the rest of you. You can inform yourselves, draw back from certain products and stop giving them your money.

9

Circles of Life

W E SPOKE about a circle of life on the farm with the crops and animals, and these small energetic circles exist in many places. You even make energy in your bodies with the citric-acid or Krebs cycle. Energy circles are more common than you think, even though they are invisible to those of you who use linear time. One of your circles is domestic and involves food preparation. The circle involves work outside the home, buying fresh food, preparing and eating it, and then hours of energetic time in the evening to enjoy friends or a hobby. That sets you up for the next day, and you don't feel that your whole life is exhaustive work followed by too-tired-to-go-out, just going to sit and watch TV again. The food itself gives you the energy to live and enjoy life. If your food doesn't make you feel good and full of energy you are not eating the right food. Some of your food is so non-nutritious that "food" is not really the right name for it.

Your lives are now so economically constricted that you feel you can't spend time or money on good quality food. Those who will not eat fresh food have chosen a lifestyle that leads to less vibrant health. The choice was made to do something else with the time and money that has less support for life. It's as if you are absent from your own lives, and you are blinded to the effect of the choices you are making. Because you are asked to work such long hours you can't stop to live and enjoy your lives. This is a new planet and you have the chance for everything to be new, if you don't like something that is hanging over from 2012, change it. Situations that happened on the old Earth do not have to be carried forward. Many, many things came to an end in December 2012.

What does that advice mean in practice? If you have job and you don't enjoy it, do you have to keep doing it? Not if you can spend some time seriously thinking about how you would like to live instead. This is a time for creating the life you want to live, for making big plans and thinking about the steps you need to take put them into place. The energy of the new Earth will support plans that are good for you, and it's ready to help everyone. It won't help those who do not take action to move forward. This is a time for trusting and recognising opportunities when they arrive.

Improved crop yields have led to higher population growth around the world as more and more children survive and lead to larger families. This could make us sound like we don't care if children die young, but we see it from a different point of view from you on the ground. We see one soul splitting itself into many smaller and smaller pieces, and each person struggling to have a pleasant life. A few of you could live on a green planet with fertile fields surrounded by animals or oceans full of fish. Up until a few centuries' ago this is how life was for many of you. There were lessons to learn about money, happiness and servitude, but for many now life has come to mean a day-long search for the next meal. Many have put aside all other considerations and all other learning opportunities to find enough food for the family. If you are part of the affluent West you do not see this, but the rest of the world is full of hungry people. Famine is more than a news story to them. You came here to learn about yourselves in a complicated but beautiful classroom. This kind of food poverty slows down the learning process even farther. You have an opportunity to learn through famine about sharing and compassion.

The Earth is a planet that supports a multitude of life. Large mono-culture farms sprayed with pesticides are approaching the status of inland deserts for the lack of variety and species of life that are present. Life gives off energy and the old methods of farming had a lot of inter-species energy. Did you ever think that insects might miss you? Or that the Earth designed a lively surface full of life and now it was very quiet and lonely? The Earth is sentient and can feel the changes on her surface and this is one change she did not intend. She didn't intend to be left alone and ignored. The balance of many species living their lives weaving around each other and interacting was part of her original plan. She hosts games for others to learn, and this time the game often involves different species finding a way to live together and appreciate one another. Through interaction she allows life to seek balance, completeness and wholeness. By comparing yourself to other people you may reach a greater understanding of yourself. The opportunity is here to expand your self-knowledge beyond your own species, and to get to know yourselves by understanding others, including the planet.

You are more than seventy years away from the small farms of the 1930s in the UK, and during those years you have learned to farm animals intensively for meat. Packed into small unnatural pens and cages they live short and unhappy lives as objects, the meat for your meals. The sadness of these animals becomes part of you when you eat them. Have you ever noticed how unhappy people are in some countries?

There can be a lot of grumbling and complaining. One of the causes is that you are eating animals that hold sadness; it's as if the meat is drenched in sadness. You wouldn't want spoiled or parasitical meat, but you will take on their unhappiness. Those who stand up for free range animals are correct, and the increase in the price of meat is fair when they are treated as you would like to be treated yourselves. If you eat less meat as a result it will still be enough when the meal is filled out with vegetables.

The old farms held a variety of animals and poultry and the farmer was a multi-skilled man who knew how to care for each type of animal. He looked after them, growing their food as well as food for people. The circle was complete in many farms, and there was harmony present when animals contributed to the overall production of food. It may have been low-tech by today's standards, but it worked in many variations across the world. The food produced by these farms contained balance and the energy of wholeness. There was nothing missing from the circle to create low-energy food. When people eat food that is produced healthily and with love, then those are the qualities that are absorbed by eating. You are what you eat.

Food today is attractive and looks perfect, but it has sometimes been produced in an artificial manner. Cucumbers are grown in tubes to stop them curling, making them easy to ship. If you saw a bent one you could think something was wrong with it, but cucumbers are not a straight vegetable. You are offered fruit and vegetables that are blemish free and attractive, but they rarely look that way by accident. They are coaxed into a shape that will sell easily, picked before they are ripe and shipped to you to buy. It is possible to send your awareness into a stack of fruit and ask yourself 'On a scale of 0 – 10, what do

I feel is the energy of this particular fruit?' If you keep doing this you will find it easier to come up with a number, you will become quicker and more confident, and it will help to guide you in decision making. It's actually impossible for you to not be able to tell the energy of anything on the planet; you are just out of practice. Irradiated fruit and vegetables that never spoil in your refrigerators will have zero energy.

The food you chose to eat every day should be freshly picked, organic without chemicals, naturally raised, not microwaved or irradiated, and ideally grown by someone who loves growing it. If you make this your way of eating you will evolve into a person who knows when to stop eating, craves freshness, and builds a stronger immune system. Your immune system when functioning in an optimal manner helps you to avoid catching the common cold more than once every three or four years, and to stave off some of the killing conditions that people fall prey to at the moment. Having an occasional cold strengthens your immune system, but catching every cold that other people have shows that your immune system is weak. A strong immune system is able to halt some serious illnesses and conditions in their tracks, although some people manifest these conditions as part of their life plan. At the moment we see many elderly people who are ill and drugged with prescription drugs, and this is a distortion of what you all wanted for yourselves as you aged. You didn't plan an experience on Earth that ended unhappily with you becoming helpless or ill.

The elderly and infirm among you provide a way for you to demonstrate love and allows you to care for others. However, if you enter a care home where the bodies are there but the minds of the elderly are medicated you may see the very strange case of bodies with billowing, drifting souls that are barely attached to the original body. As long as they are attached the souls do not leave and the person does not die. Death is now so feared that people will hang on to their lives, even if it does not look like a very happy life to outsiders. All of these people hanging onto life around the world add to the total of unhappiness and fear. We would love for you to let go of your fear of death. It is safe to die, and then you can understand everything you learned in this life and plan for a new life. There are not too many elderly people on the planet, there are only too many who are sick or in pain. It's all so unnecessary.

We are talking about the care of elderly people in the same section as animals because there are similarities in the way they are treated in Western societies. They are separated from the rest of society and put into homes by themselves. We see so much sadness in these homes, and people are imprisoned in their rooms and buildings a little like farm animals in pens, and kept away out of sight. The best of these homes foster a community spirit and people are happy, the worst can only exist because the rest of you turn a blind eye to what it is like inside them. This is a case of not seeing yourselves as one human soul, and ignoring those in a poorly run home. These homes are a violation of the golden rule 'Treat others as you wish to be treated yourself.'

The elderly are a great reservoir of experience and life, and they used to be respected as wise men and women. This has changed in the last sixty years or so, and now your world leaders are young men with young families. They lack experience because they were not alive at an age to remember when important events were taking place. Youthful energy is valued over experience for the first time in your long history.

There are so many reasons for this change; there is a cult of youth you see reflected in advertising and entertainment, and the top positions in Western industrial countries are expected to be very intense with little time off. Some wonder if an old man could do this job successfully. People are reluctant to be reminded of past mistakes that could be repeated, because everything is said to be better now and we are protected from hardships by our elected leaders. Experience is not valued, youth, money and promises are.

Sometimes when we write it sounds as if you could only turn the clock back you would find everything was fine, but that is not what we mean. You cannot turn the clock back and everything in the world was not perfect then. Crops were grown by people who starved even while they worked for the landowner, as in the great Chinese famines of the 1950s and 60s. We are only looking in this book at the energy of the food you eat. The energy of anything you take into your body should be as whole as possible. There is a lot of low-energy food eaten, and even nutritional supplements vary in the amount of energy they contain. Everything you eat of low energy must be subsidised by your own energy to make it good for you and to keep you healthy. The only way around this is to draw universal energy into you to help you be full to the brim, and there are many people who either use Reiki on their food to bring up its energy levels, or treat themselves daily, or both. Many people wonder how something as simple as Reiki, or Universal Life Force energy can help anyone, and part of the way it helps is by keeping your energy levels high so your body works optimally. Reiki is a top-quality healing energy of light.

The rebirth of the Earth has changed the energy of the

planet, and there is light rising up into your bodies. Many people have had colds and flu as the light rises and cleans through them. It's a fine, high energy, one that makes it harder for germs to live in your bodies. It also makes it less comfortable for any one who desires to live in the shadows. The new Earth energy is a gift for those who align with the light for wellness, for insight and for spirituality.

10

The Earth's Role in Balancing Food Production

T HE EARTH controls the weather and she provides different conditions for life. One of the major conditions is the current slant of the Earth's axis. There have been many predictions elsewhere that the Earth's axis will right itself, and this process is already underway in a gentle manner. The tilt provides long days of sunlight in the Northern Hemispheres and is relied on to ripen certain crops such as English strawberries and Scottish raspberries. But change is coming and part of it will be to straighten up the axis and change the growing conditions. The tilted axis was part of the old Earth and the straight one is part of the new Earth.

The tilted axis of the Earth unbalances her, and she travels around the sun tipped half-way over. She was unable to right herself before now, but she intends to straighten up again in the next generation or so. The animals will stretch and say 'Balance at last', but humans will be shocked. They will have to relearn living on a balanced Earth and with the changes in sunlight hours. The two poles and the nearest land to them will grow colder. Europe will still have green summers but many people will migrate towards the equators. This could sound like a disaster movie, except it is already written in as part of the plot that the population will decline in a natural manner. People will begin to have fewer children. The effect on which food is grown and where it is grown will be tremendous. There is a difference in human time and Earth time, and her perception of speed is different than ours. Straightening up in the first twenty-five years of a 26,000 year cycle seems very fast to her.

Because you have not lived on a balanced Earth for many years you have a distant relationship with her. You will have to relearn how to live with her when she is upright once again. Regaining her balance and aligning her axis is the final step to clicking back into place with the rest of the universe. That will be the single biggest change of all (written about in *And I Saw a New Earth*).

The new Earth brings with it a strong impetus for change, but if all the changes happened overnight it could do more harm than good. The first few years are going to set up the conditions for the next 26,000 years. Humanity's role in this is to help by choosing how they want to live. We are hoping that everyone will think about what would suit them and put their energy into creating happy lives. Imagine a planet intent on change with a population on its surface holding on to the vanished past. They could make a new world with a lot of attributes of the old world. If you feel that life could be better for you there will have to be changes, and by thinking about your own life and what would make you happy helps you adjust. Holding on to the past will find you unable to move with the times. It was never as important as now to let go.

There will only be a few years to tear down some of the existing structures of politics and economies before building anew, depending on where you live in the world. In some nations it will take longer, and in others it will flow easily and the local people will barely change their ways. It depends on where they started from. You can make this as hard on yourselves as you like, but we recommend letting go of the detritus of the old world and moving with the planet. It is her role and her intention to look after you.

Political and Financial Changes 2013 to 2015

11

The Energy of Taxes

BECAUSE everything is changing now, the established political systems across the world will also begin to change. Today countries can have populations in the millions with relatively few people in the central governments. Many of the decisions taken by politicians on behalf of local areas can be counter-productive. People are once again in the position of working for others, this time to earn enough money for taxes and it's very hard to change this situation. A typical and modern example is the European Union, which was created as a layer of government above the national governments. It was decided the E.U. needed a budget and taxes were established, and the E.U. Parliament chooses how to spend the money.

Think about whom is taking advantage of your labour and the associated energy of enforced slavery, the unhappiness of slaves and the lack of light present in those who live off the work of others. This is not an easy problem to unravel.

Being a government employee does not mean one is enslaving others, but the institution of government itself imposes a lack of choice once the government is elected.

In the beginning of civic government men came together to organise services such as schools and fire fighting. These days it's been forgotten what tax is for or how to use it. Taxes are to pay for services that benefit the whole community such as roads and hospitals. You live in communities of people, send your tax money away to the centre and have little say in how it is spent locally. This isn't just about taxes; involvement in your own community strengthens it and you stop being a powerless bystander. The community stands a better chance of getting what it needs when local people participate in organising and choosing services.

There are many reasons why this does not happen already, including the fact that you are all so busy that it is a relief to hand any job over to someone else. Your lives are not balanced. We're talking about working alongside others and taking responsibility for the community and environment you live in. This isn't about service to others so much as helping yourselves by making local choices, sharing and joining together. You are one soul and every action that brings you closer together is going in the right direction.

In the past you tried different forms of government, and many of you in the West belong to systems where you each vote for someone to represent you in the capital. In democracies you are often represented by one person, and many of these representatives do not fully devote themselves to the electorate. For representatives in many countries it has become a very lucrative career with high rewards. The representative becomes distanced from those who elected them, and most of the time is spent with their new colleagues in the capital and not with the electorate. Developing their own interests and career connections within their new community of elected representatives is normal, and they jostle for position among themselves. They haven't forgotten their constituencies, but they no longer consort with them. It's become two-tiered, with the electorate one step further away. Once in power they can be lost to those who elected them.

Today your representatives are the ones who have the greatest influence on how tax money is spent locally. This is one of the main reasons you are represented, to divide up the taxes that were collected. Their own financial interests are tied in with their new position, and their decisions for the rest of you can be based on trade-offs with other representatives. These are some of the conversations we sometimes refer to as taking place behind closed doors. In the end you are told that jobs or money are not coming your way, but you rarely know the real reason why.

Politics today, from a dictatorship to democracy exploits the common man in large part due to this central pot of money paid in taxation. Over half of all the money earned by the middle classes in the UK is paid to the government in taxes. How many millions of middle class workers are earning money, and how much are they paying every year? Who among them does not contribute through a large variety of individual taxes, income tax, national insurance or VAT? This is at least half of a whole nation's earned income paid in taxes with those paying it having very little say in how it is spent. Non-tax payers and corporations receive the taxes, and the wealthiest classes hire accountants to reduce their tax bills. Large corporations gain government contracts that pay them to provide services, often paying very little tax internationally while profiting from the contracts. Taxes are paid when earned and again when they are spent. It adds up to more tax than any government will admit to demanding.

Some of the welfare and benefit programmes provided by the central government prevent people from being responsible for themselves. We are looking here at just the energy resulting from taxation. Angels do not pay taxes, and we do not promote any political party. But we do see the effect of the energy on the people who pay, and on the people who receive. Paying taxes has become a crushing burden, and there is very little choice in the amount paid and where the money goes. Receiving tax money for support helps a person to not fully engage with life or fulfil their potential. They are denied the chance to get everything possible out of life. It also allows others to not personally help out of kindness. Tax payers do not always follow through to see who the money is being given to. Not every recipient of tax money is made happy by it, and therefore they are not getting much happiness out of their lives.

The London Paralympics were the crucial part of the whole Olympic Games; they showed the disabled viewers another possibility for themselves and provided role-models. The able bodied spectators saw that these were tremendous athletes, worthy of admiration. Performing to such a high level and overcoming mental and physical disabilities was far harder for them than for some able-bodied athletes. The Olympian athletes can no longer be limited only to those who are not disabled. The healthy, hard-working athletes of the Olympic Games provide good role models for the rest of the population who are used to 'celebrities' famous for very little reason. The 2012 Olympic Games had the affect of brightening up the energy of the whole planet in the summer. Everything good that lifted the overall energy of the planet in 2012 meant that by the final days in December the new Earth was ready to start again on its 26,000 year cycle from a lighter place. It allowed you and the Earth to be reborn from an energetically different starting point, and one from where the journey to humanity's ascension could be made a bit easier for you.

Political change will come about as world events make governments irrelevant; they will be seen as expensive and ineffective when asked to solve a nation's problems. The decisions needed to help the voters will not come to pass as the government is too far away from them to really understand their lives. As they continue to govern and ask for more and more money from those who already find it hard to pay their taxes there will be an impasse, the imbalance of the status quo on the old Earth vs. new Earth, old expectations vs. reality. At the end of the day taxes can't be collected from those who cannot afford to pay them.

Tax collection and disbursement are the main functions of government. Do you agree with this statement? Can you think of anything the government does that is not paid for through your taxes? You work to give them the money, and they then should be working for you to give you only the things that need to be paid for in common. This is not what is happening, and part of the problem is that there is so much money available that programs are begun to use some of the money, then they are never discontinued and become a part of what government is expected to do. We are tackling an emotive subject by talking about taxes, which implies politics to many and we have a suggestion: really focus and concentrate on what is for the highest good of all.

Let's say someone is a welfare recipient and does not work nor pay taxes but is given money to live. Will that person live long enough on that money to learn how to be happy? If so perhaps it is a good use of the money. A happy person will return your investment to you by spreading joy. It's a genuine case of buying joy with money. It is not a good investment of your money if welfare recipients are never joyful, but lack joy through being underused by society. Knowing that society has no use for you does not tend to make one truly happy, but having a purpose in life does. Removing all purpose from life so that a person is fed, sheltered and entertained without any opportunity to work gives a false impression of happiness. People were not born on Earth to be numbed to the experience of life. In addition, large concentrations of unhappy people living together do not help to raise the vibration for the rest of you, as you can't escape the effects of human unhappiness when you are all one.

How will you solve the problem of high taxes and too many other people relying on government money? This is a trick question because you will have this problem solved for you when your economies readjust over the years through 2015. There are many unfair aspects to your economic systems right now, and your governments have gone as far as they could in the old ways. After the pendulum has swung so far it reverses direction. This is not something that has been done to you by others; this is how you act because you don't remember you are all one. From our point of view you are all one soul divided into separate bodies, from your point of view you are individuals and only loosely connected.

Individualism is highly valued but the reason for individualism has been forgotten: it is a way to collect more experiences for your greater soul. How difficult you have made your journey towards ascension!

Which areas of finance, money and taxes need to be corrected? In different countries there have been news articles and demonstrations about who is paying tax and who is not. These issues are beginning to be talked about, but what will correct these situations and how long will it take? We're saying to hold on tight, because the corrections look like they are going to happen within three years in many countries. The new Earth's energy is very different, and when the underlying feeling to everything is 'Stop! Enough is enough' then change will begin to happen rapidly.

Change has always taken place on Earth, but in the past you had time to consider what is happening and choose how you want to deal with it. This is going to change to a rapid pace as the energy supporting the old system is no longer here. Those of you who go wholeheartedly with the new Earth energy will turn your faces towards the future and not look back at the past at all. The past is over, and all the systems already in place will change so that it is fairer for everyone. By this point you may be wondering if you will live on this new Earth or if you are one of the people who did not choose to come. If you are reading this book you chose to leave the old behind and make a life on the new.

We talked a lot about planets and their role of hosting games for other soul groups in *Planet Earth Today*. Would a planet, as a being of light, abandon over 50% of the population to die? Planets are very special and loving, and not into killing off their guests if they can avoid it. In this instance, having made it to her renewal date of December 2012 she has carefully considered her own needs, and is emitting a stronger presence. People can tell that she is stronger by watching the news and weather reports. Where there are natural disasters, are they good for the Earth, or are they good for people? Sometimes the answer to both questions is yes, but it is better to wait and see the final outcomes over time. These days the results could come more quickly, and you need to consider the after affects of the disaster. When something terrible happens you would benefit from following the story to the very end and see what has been the overall result. What if everyone decided not to burn more fossil fuel and the result was that people stayed closer to home? How would that affect the planet and families? Training yourself to see the bigger picture is part of the growth of your soul, becoming one with other humans and one with all of life.

In financial changes the ultimate goal is to make everyone happy. Remember this as the changes start, and use the intuition you have developed through practice. You will be looking for go-ahead energy attached to any possible investment or new employer. Already there is a difference to the sound of voices as people from the old Earth speak on the news. They speak without energy and once you begin to hear this you will lose interest in what they are saying. It's worth exercising your skills at detecting energy; all of you are able to do this. Many do this now on an unconscious level.

You allowed a political and financial system to be erected in your names that causes misery in day-to-day lives. It needs to be swept away before the new society can have space to form. It will be like a cliff crumbling and sliding down hill until there is nothing left but boulders, and there will be a backlash and rebuilding, but society is unlikely to reproduce anything as cruel again. When the financial systems slide downhill you will not find yourselves back in the dark ages, we have said elsewhere you don't need to repeat that experience. You will be somewhere new, ready to have new experiences. If you have a toothache you will still go to a dentist or to a bank if you need to borrow money for a new house or business. This time choose your business associations by reading their energy. You are already able to recognise who you wish to do business with or who to avoid based on how they feel, you just need to practice and act on your instincts.

The old financial system developed to make money for the top level of executives, then the owners and shareholders. This is already considered by many to be unacceptable in 2013, and as it was learned that tax money was being used to top up the salaries of those workers on minimum wages, it put these firms into vulnerable positions. Firms need people to buy their goods, but without the goodwill of the public there will suddenly be no buyers. You should not be asked to pay taxes so that large corporations can use your money to pay their employees a living wage, just as you should not contribute to over-large bonuses. This is only one example of the government taking an action in your name that makes you very angry when found out.

In a democracy what are your choices? You are able to vote in elections and carry on with the same system. You could abstain and not vote. Do you think the government will cease to exist if few people vote? The country will be ruled by the party with the most votes, just like today. So what are your choices for bringing about change? Happily you have some brave examples from two great human beings, both born in South Africa: Nelson Mandela and the Mahatma Gandhi. Mandela held steady in the face of violence and did not behave in the same manner as the previous governments. He acted with love towards friend and foe alike and he made an impossible hate-filled situation fizzle out. Instead of streets running with blood he led his country to free elections and avoided a painful civil war. Gandhi also led a campaign of non-violence against the ruling country, and in the end Britain withdrew. India was handed back to Indians for self-governance. Gandhi organised marches and protests but when they were opposed by the police and soldiers the protestors did not strike back. In the end the world was so appalled that the rulers were forced out.

The Earth's support has been withdrawn from any corrupt world governments and these will need human support to stay in place. Your energy will keep them going, or you can turn away. All governments exist because the people keep them in place.

In the UK at the moment there is a blockage in the normal progression of family life as young people cannot afford to leave the parental home and set up new families. They cannot get employment, earn down payments on a house or pay mortgages. They can't get married or afford to have babies. If they do manage part of this ladder they look forward to years of heavy mortgage payments where a couple needs to work very hard just for shelter. And yet, people support the current political system with their energy, and they keep it in place.

One of the reasons for writing our books is that we don't want people to be paralysed by the fear of what's coming in the future. What reason other than fear would make people support systems that don't serve them? We are talking about a three year period of 'society turning upside down'. At the end of that time there will be a level playing field as some fall down and others rise up. Think of a tower struck by lightening and crumbling flat to the ground, and the people at the top of the tower mix with everyone else at ground level. What would this mean to you in your profession, especially if you are disabled or a woman? Some jobs always go to the same few people, but your talent pool is much wider than that. Many young people without family connections see no way to rise up the employment ladder.

12

Living Locally

IN THREE years an entire generation of young people could walk away from society and begin living very different lives from the one their parents lived. They could opt out of the job and housing market, etc. and take their children with them. These will be the first families to live balanced lives with some work, growing their own food, and raising their own children in smaller homes while enjoying more family time. They will not have the stress of trying to live inside an economic system where everything is already owned by someone else. It's not giving up, it's deciding to walk away and live more flexible lives.

These families will form communities where there is work and play, and where the children are guided by their parents as they grow up. They will find space to live away from the big urban centres and the Earth will be more evenly populated. The endless drift to the cities will be reversed and there will be more medium-sized towns. The first people to do this will find it very natural to live this way. They will be leaving a society that has nothing to offer them in the way of using their skills and talents. These young people will be happy and content and others will notice, particularly their children. By the time their children have grown up they will be content with visits to the city for arts and sport. It all sounds very idyllic. This scenario depends on the availability of land to purchase, work, and transport options. Schools, shops, work, it sounds like a return to the 1880's.

However you won't be going back to the 1880's; people have already lived through those years. But what can you take from that earlier society that increases the level of happiness that each person has in their life? Back then there were healthy people surrounded by extended families, and their connections in life were based on family love and loyalty rather than corporate loyalty. Surrounded by friends and family they felt they had allies in life, people who would help them when they needed help. They didn't need to worry about their personal fate as people do today. They worked hard all day long and looking back you may think 'no thank you', but they were happy people and they didn't expect so much leisure time. Leisure time is the part of the day when you do what you like, but they enjoyed their whole day. Even in the Dark Ages people were happier than you are now.

Today you are disconnected from helping others by giving money either to a charity or in your taxes. Giving money allows you to deny (in some cases) how bad off the people really are that you are helping. Philanthropy allows others to be hired to assist needy people, but it insulates the giver from a personal and emotional connection to others. It makes it harder to see yourselves as one soul and one species and is taking a backwards step.

What we suggest is that you role up your sleeves and help others locally. You could donate some time to helping others in addition to your money. It's a two-way process: they get helped and you have an opportunity to learn you are all one. Can you see how this works in a circle? Your local community has people that need help, you help them and your community becomes a better place as you learn how to live together. Your worries ease over what would happen to you if you needed help one day, knowing that there are people ready to step forward and help out of love. This would be a very large change to take place!

Somehow humans forgot that happiness was something worth having, and focused on money instead. It was as if the entire world began to do this. We are not aiming this book at the few who have more money than they can spend in a lifetime, but at the overwhelming majority of people. You want to be like the wealthy because you believe money will make you happy. There are so many moments of happiness in your lives that have nothing to do with spending a lot of money. You are happy because you are laughing with children or friends, or you are outside and it's a nice day. One thing that makes you sink into unhappiness is stress, and then you have trouble raising your spirits again.

Stress is universal among humanity now, except among those who have walked away from the rat race. The more primitive the person the happier they tend to be. Many of you will feel stressed as your financial systems start to steadily collapse. You will see the money in stock markets losing value and worry that you will have nothing left. Removing it you may put it into another form of investment like land, but that begins to decline as all investments begin to fail. You worry about your pension values. This is what we are talking about, stress and worry but most of all it's about not believing that you will always be looked after. All anyone needs is a warm home and enough food to live, and the extras that make for happiness are about being with people. What if you never worried about how much money you had? Could you replace that worry with contentment with what you do have? How can others have enough if what's here isn't shared between all of you? Now the Earth itself is supplying the energy for change. When you know you are all one you will not stand by and see another part of yourself die of starvation.

The Earth's role in all of this is to initiate change by providing energy in the form of light to get you back on track. You came here to learn about yourselves as a part of God, and fewer and fewer people are leading the kind of life that will allow this to happen. You are too busy, and too misinformed to make any progress in learning who you are. Once again, as in the days before Atlantis, you are like ants swarming aimlessly in the summer's heat. Earth promised humanity the space to learn along with her help. This is her opportunity to gently close off some pathways and guide you to others. She did not do this before, but in this renewal of herself she became a new planet, one who chose the qualities she needed to survive and help you achieve your original desire. You did not expect this help and we hope you will find yourselves less distracted and able to move in a straight line towards ascension.

The human soul can not buy their ascension with money. The energy of money today needs to go back to its original level and play a part in your societies that is not swollen out of all recognition. It is like a stream that has burst its banks and everyone must concentrate on it not to get swept away. It can return to being a stream again and being part of a balanced system. Money is above all a servant, and should not be the master in your lives.

Sometimes change can happen very quickly as it did in 2011 at Fukushima in Japan. One minute there were people and towns, and the next minute they were washed away and a nuclear power station was damaged. There isn't always a lot of notice in advance of change, sometimes it just happens. People think that it's very hard to change and worry about doing it, but you are actually able to change very easily. You are very adaptable, and can change quickly when you need to. If your world changed in three years you would say that was shockingly fast, that you needed time to consider your own futures and prepare for them. But if you were not given the time you would adjust anyway, and it would be far easier than you thought. To go with the flow of energy, even the energy of change, is far easier than trying to hang on to something that is finished. Change is not something to be worried about.

You are going to see changes that you never thought you would see in your lifetimes. The financial markets will not be gone entirely but shrunken to the point where they no longer act as a casino, but simply as a means of raising money for businesses. Once they reach their new level you will see a genuine value and use for such a market. Speculating in stocks and shares to make more money has no use other than to make money for somebody, but not necessarily for the company whose name is on the stock, although the stock price is reflected in the strength of the company.

Financial readjustment to a fairer system would be a more accurate way to think about the times that are coming. It wasn't so many decades ago when the markets heated up and crashed in 1929. They shrank and many people suffered loss, but you came back stronger than ever. We see you as parts of your higher soul, we know that many individuals suffered greatly at that time, but your soul is still here. Once again you have shaky markets following a period of overheating, and again some will suffer while it is being rebalanced. You know that investments can go down as well as up, and there is no foolproof method of avoiding loss. Will your lovely country homes be as desirable if you can't afford the fuel to drive to them? This is what we mean by fast changes, so fast that you may be left with losses, stocks of no value or houses selling for less than you paid for them.

So what can you do? Understand that no matter what happens you are always looked after and you don't have to worry. Earth is a planet of life and living. The energy is available here to pick yourselves up and keep moving, and lead you towards anything that makes you happy.

13

The Burden of Taxation

POLITICAL changes can be quite violent and extreme as in the Arab Spring in 2011, but what took place in those countries was necessary. Can you conceive of the anger that led to that level of fighting if you did not live through it yourself? It is not necessary to have an armed rebellion every time the people are unhappy, but all countries are ripe for changing to a simpler form of government.

What happens in your lives to keep you from feeling this anger towards your own government? There is a level of misinformation and secrecy that keeps you from finding out what they are doing. That type of information is just starting to be revealed now, how a government is pressed from every direction by special interest groups or big businesses asking for favours. Remember the size of that tax pot of money. This is a whole industry in itself, how to get some of that money for your own group or company, or to make sure the laws of the land don't harm your profits.

Elected representatives oversee the spending of tax money. The United States uses the congressional committee of Ways and Means and hands lump sums to the other arms of the government such as the military, etc. The lump sums are applied for and an agreement is reached. Once that money is sent to a department it is not overseen to the same degree, unless there is a government audit. These departments have their spending plans and not every penny will be accounted for to the taxpayer. As the departments do not earn the money themselves they are removed from the care that you take when spending your own money that you've worked for. There are some existing regulations that ensure the taxes are not always spent wisely, that have been passed into law by your representatives. When you look at the energy of democratically elected governments it is as if they are cut loose from the countries they govern, and they are now detached and floating with a life of their own. This is what you feel as you complain about governments regardless of the country you live in. There is the feeling that something is living off your earnings that has nothing to do with you. In the past that was called slavery. The energy of slavery is sorrow and unfairness, anger against the one who enslaved you, and a feeling of rebellion. Slavery has no place on Earth, it is not seeing the enslaved as the same as yourself, and it is not treating others as you would like to be treated yourself.

As you can imagine, there are variations of popular uprisings but we would be sorry to see anyone pick up arms and attack anyone else. Neither would we like to see a host of non-tax payers in prison. How can change bring about the kind of government that is connected to the people? We're not saying this sounds enjoyable in the short term, but if no one has any money to pay their taxes what will happen? There is already a borrowing crisis where governments have to pay higher and higher interest rates to get more money for their budgets. The interest payments on the borrowed money can be crippling for a nation as in the cases of Greece and Italy, for example. If tax revenues fall because the economy shrinks, governments can't tax the people even more, just when they have no spare cash. This isn't the time of King John and Robin Hood.

One of the big differences today is that people are connected through the internet and they exchange ideas and news. The reason information is spreading quickly now is that once it appears online others can share it quite easily. There are people reading original documents on the web that very few would have been able to read before, and once something is revealed online it spreads like wildfire as it did in the case of the wikileaks. Not all of the information that appears is about the government, some people are researching large corporations and although not every document is available on the internet it is harder to keep secrets now than ever before. Angels don't like secrets, either it is open and beneficial to share, or it is the opposite. Secretive people tend not to have everyone else's highest good as a priority.

The language of science is often English, and the planet is full of English speakers at the moment (although there are also just as many Spanish and Chinese speakers.) The primary military and industrial nations are English speaking, and the international language of arms manufacture, pharmaceuticals, popular music and films, and much of computer use is in English. Currently there is a great opening-up of information, friendships and contacts taking place across the globe. People are beginning to get to know others around the world as individuals, meeting online and sometimes going on to marry someone from a foreign country. There are fewer barriers now to making new friends internationally than ever before. Once you know someone there's a better chance you will see their point of view in an argument. You can hear their stories first hand without someone else editing them.

Looking ahead there is a period of chaos as money becomes scarcer. This is already happening. It will start at the bottom as people simply stop buying anything that does not keep them alive. Those who are wealthy and are looking to sell to mass markets will find no one is buying and factories and shops are closing. Their income is decreased as the return on their investments decrease. People also no longer wish to buy so many expensive items. Everyone seems to be asking for money, from insurance companies to fuel companies to health providers.

Take the insurance industry as an example. There are people who will stop buying insurance and hope that they never need it. The Earth will continue to provide floods, droughts, earthquakes and volcanoes. Large insurance companies will try to meet their obligations to those who bought insurance, and find they are putting their fees up and up, beyond what anyone feels they can afford. Stocks and shares in the insurance industry begin to lose money as profits decrease. This is an example of how it could happen in industry after industry. Ultimately what we see is a level playing field for people, and as they become closer economically they become closer once again. The lack of empathy with the poorest people in the world shows you how far you are from feeling one with them.

It sounds like everything will be destroyed! Not destroyed but changed, and changed for the better if you become closer and more human. In the end you will have a new society for a new planet, one where people have shorter working days doing jobs they love. This used to be enough for all of you before you felt that money was the object of your working lives. It was only in the last century that the general population felt they needed all the money they could acquire, and you left the pathway of happiness and started walking on a dead-end street. It didn't matter how much money one had, in surveys the answer was always that everyone would like to have a little more. People were afraid that they wouldn't have enough to take care of themselves in old age. The world is changing towards light, and that means happiness and no more fear. Money failed to make the overwhelming number of people happy, and fear is not a sustainable base for life.

We feel torn between telling you the truth and trying to allay your fears about what is coming. Humanity is going for a wild ride on the back of a tiger. This is the leap downward, and it will be followed by the leap upward. You can shed the old habits that keep you enslaved to money, and you can bounce back up and be happy if you keep in mind happiness as your goal. This is about flow and flow is connected to the universe like an electric cord plugged in to the wall. Flow contains the energy to carry you along from one place to the next, but if the power is turned off you have to do all the work yourself. Trust the flow to carry you forward and it will do exactly that, and you will travel forward and not backwards.

New Patterns of Living 2013 to 2040

14

Receiving the Gifts of the Universe

LET'S LOOK at your current patterns of living: there are great numbers of people living together in cities around the world, and parents are struggling to have enough money for food and housing. The parents are either both working hard all day and not raising their children themselves, or they are home in receipt of welfare or benefits. By the time people have children they try to earn as much as they can to buy food, clothing, shelter and transport. Fortunately many earn enough to provide this. There are also many who receive money from the government for these items, but they never receive enough for them to live in luxury. You may resent that some people are living off your tax money, but if you spent a week in their shoes you would wish wholeheartedly for a change that allowed everyone to live a life that had some meaning.

One of the problems for humanity is the current drift to cities to work for others. This began as people felt they would be better off living there. Some young people felt bored in the country, and other's thought they worked too hard for their money locally and that life would be easier in the city. Life in large cities appears of poor quality to us, away from the Earth and living in apartments or small homes, you appear to be working hard without the rewards of a pleasant life or clean air and water. Those who rise early for their work and arrive home late have little time for leisure. On weekends they're busy catching up with everything they didn't have time for all week. What's missing for humanity is a place to live where the journey to work is very quick, the pay is sufficient for their needs, and the hours are shorter. Young people living and working in cities can make sense, as does moving away from them when they have children. When we watch all of you in cities you seem to lack life, you tend to drain each other's energy through over-crowding and competition for space and income, and find it harder to connect to the Earth. Few city workers get outdoors for more than their lunch hour. To find living space for the many people currently in the cities to move away there will have to be changes in land ownership, and changes in the birth rate. The time has ended for overpopulation and for a system where a few people own everything. The energy no longer supports either of these and has now changed.

Growth of new towns will lead the changes over the coming decades. In the past in Great Britain, new towns were imposed by government planners as a ring of towns around London. The future new towns will spread organically across many countries when there is migration away from the big cities. People will be looking for a place that gives them a good life and where they won't need to travel to a dull job.

Where once workers flooded into large cities all around the world, the lack of jobs in those same cities will push them out again. Those with families will be able to live and work with mixed careers in small or medium sized towns and villages. The Earth has a lot of space, but at the moment people are concentrated in the cities while the countryside is comparatively empty. Populations will begin to spread more evenly across the empty spaces.

Right now the countryside is all owned by individuals or the government. In order for people to move to new areas to live there will have to be very large changes indeed; perhaps as large as suspending belief in the right for one family to own a piece of the Earth. We see a living planet, and you see a piece of real estate. There have been things done to the Earth without her permission, roads have been constructed in inappropriate places, mountain tops flattened in the Appalachians for coal, and rivers constrained by dams and levees. But not everything is forbidden, and to build a house or a commercial building and then sell it is not necessarily wrong. The idea that a person owns a piece of the Earth is false. The Earth owns the Earth, just as every person should own themselves.

The Earth is designed to be in balance, with land and oceans, farmland and wild areas. People are drawn to wild areas because there are almost no man-made structures to distort the energy coming through from the planet. Those who love to walk or hike in wild areas do so because they want to be outside, challenged by the terrain and to escape from civilisation. There are places where the energy of the Earth isn't tarnished by development, and it is restful to be in these places and in full flow of the Earth's energy. There is great beauty on Earth, and many people crave being outside and close to her.

You disregard the fact that the Earth is alive and forms the biggest part of the ecosystem and therefore do not feel grateful to her for all she does for you. Gratitude is taught to children by saying or writing 'thank you.' It's only when you are older that you realise that the biggest beneficiary of gratitude is yourself. If you cannot be grateful to others for what they do for you, then your outer shell has become so hard that nothing good can penetrate. If the gifts of others fall on you like rain, would you rather be a hard pavement or a piece of loose earth? Any rain falling on a pavement evaporates easily and is gone, while rain on the earth soaks in. The energy of receiving is soft, and gratitude acknowledges that you receive gifts that are given to you freely through love. Learning to be grateful is a necessary first step to living with the Earth. If you aren't grateful to the Earth for what you receive from her, then how can you fully realise how closely connected you are to her?

The Earth has provided you with a home for quite some time and she feels sad that she is giving you gifts and they are unable to reach you. Receiving gifts comes in many different forms. For some of you there is the work you want to do, and for others it may be the place you want to live. Love is the gift that penetrates all the way to your core, and once you are replete with love you have everything. Love is the same as joy and happiness, and is the reason why we work so hard to help you find the way to be happy. Love allows you to live with yourself in harmony, and spreads into every one of your relationships. If everyone loved themselves around the world there would be an end to war and strife. Love yourself first before joining with another in partnership, and come together as equals. When two people who love themselves are together there is no shortage of love in the relationship, and no one looks for another to supply the love they do not feel for themselves. There is more to building a successful relationship such as compatibility, but loving yourself is the place to start.

Love could be the basis of your lives, but there is a lot of distortion around true love on your planet. 'I love myself enough to....' should be a regular thought. You are the person you know the best, and you are very loveable. Some people are only safe to love once you have found you love yourself, and then everyone is safe. If someone truly loved themselves, would they stay with a partner who abused them?

Some countries seem home to a certain kind of self-loathing, and some children are raised to make themselves appear small and not attract attention. You are all beautiful, beautiful people and to see those who cannot accept this, who don't think of themselves as lovely and capable, is one of the saddest sights of all. If you loved yourself, you would be certain that others also loved you. From that point onwards you would never fear the look from another's eyes, or be worried about disappointing someone else. There are those who never feel good enough, but they are the only ones who believe that about themselves. Self love is a way to love every person on the planet with all their flaws, just as you are flawed but loveable. Loving yourself is the same as loving the Creator who made you and is a part of you, and all the people that join you as one soul. If you don't love yourself first, the love you give to another is diminished.

You were born loving yourself, and then learned to fear that others did not love you. Finally we are saying you need to learn how to love yourself again; and that you are worthy of love. We angels are beings of love and light, created to express this throughout all our existence in this universe. You are also a being that has learned love and light in your long past. To believe that you are unworthy of love is an absence of belief that God is love and you are a small part of Him. On Earth the absence of love fosters darkness, lies, secrets and war. You personally can alter this by loving yourself and acting to make yourself happy. Love and happiness can spread.

Showing gratitude can be somewhat dormant in modern people. You will thank others for favours and gifts, but often it's not heartfelt. Of course some people are exceptions, and as they feel gratitude their energy softens and that allows more gifts to come to them. There is a lot of talk about how to attract abundance into your lives, and heartfelt gratitude is a good place to start. The Earth, the universe and your Creator gives to every person and every life form good things, only to watch them slide off from a hard outer surface. Can abundance be as easy as being grateful for everything you are given all day long? Try noticing how you feel when you are grateful, beginning with the Earth, air and water and then moving on to other things. Train yourselves to be grateful, and to stop and notice what's really important in your world.

Gratitude is a way to take you out of yourselves and consider the person who considered you and gave you a gift. When you really think about this other person you spread your consciousness out from your own life to that of another. If someone else cares enough to give you something, then think how limitless the rest of the universe is, and how you could be receiving good things without limit. The universe is waiting to hear from you to find out what you would like.

Using clarity you can draw to you whatever you desire. If you act only after thinking through what exactly you want, your outward message is clear and it is easier for the universe to respond. (The universe is the total of all life, and the consciousness of all life to the farthest star. In *And I Saw A New Earth* we described God as a beach and humanity as a grain of sand. All the grains of sand make up the Creator and each grain carries the qualities of the Creator. Something can be a small part of a whole and yet enjoy all the same qualities. Humanity = the universe = God.) You need to consider what the gifts of the universe are likely to be. It is more likely to put you in the way of creating money rather than give you actual money. The important part is to be clear and not muddled. If you think that you have time to see ten clients a week that is much clearer than asking for 'a lot of clients.' You would know if you could see ten clients by carefully considering how long it took to prepare for them and see them, and what else you needed time for in your week. When you spend time thinking about your needs before asking you increase the accuracy and chances of success. When you are ready, you have a word with the universe along the lines of 'I am ready to have ten clients a week at ...... per session.' Sometimes this can work so well it is uncanny. Setting your intentions is how the universe knows what to give you.

There are going to be a few years in the near future when politicians and others find they have trouble making headway with new plans and ideas. They are living on the old Earth for the most part and trying to plan and build on a vanished planet, whilst you can make plans for yourself that include the new Earth and move forward with ease. The main thing is to formulate your intentions for the rest of your life (although these do not need to be set in stone) and put plans into action. The power to act will have moved from their hands into yours, and you may never choose to act as they do now. Politicians are eager to play a role in running countries, but they may never realise their supporting energy could vanish and leave them powerless. If the power has shifted to the people standing firmly on the new planet, then they have the power to block any acts that are not for everyone's highest good.

The same old actions will be repeated by those who did not choose to move forward onto the new Earth. If it helps you to understand, think about a ghost in a movie, they are often present but can't quite grab hold of an object or influence events. You do not have to let the people who did not choose to move forward onto the new Earth run everything from now on. Think of the people who are taking all the action in a movie while the ghost stands and watches. This is who you are, the people in the scene who are alive and taking action. You may be living with one of the 'ghost' people and realise that they are not ghosts, but are very much alive. When you close your eyes can you feel their energy in the room? If you look at their energy is it non-existent? A being without energy is a being without power. More than half of your planet is made up of people who have no energy. It is the beginning of the Earth's next cycle and they chose not to come along, and these people are here and not here at the same time. As this galactic cycle moves on they will weaken and become frustrated, and will not be grounded on the Earth. Don't let any of these people make a plan to spoil your lives or your planet, but stand in their way. Success will encourage you to more activity. Right now, do everything you can do to block plans that are not for the highest good of all, as it gives you one less thing to put right later.

15

Co-Existing with Animals

THERE ARE cultures that tend the land and live on it while giving thanks, such as the Australian Aborigine. This type of relationship is completely different from the one in the West, a complete about-face from the attitude in Europe and the USA. If you currently own a house, could you do this with the knowledge that although you bought the land surrounding your home it does not belong to you? And if you are beholden to the Earth for the land under your house on it would be nice to acknowledge it. In the West every parcel of land has an owner and profits from the ownership of the land. If you look at the history of England after the Norman Conquest in 1066 the entire country belonged to William the Conqueror, and he handed out large estates to the friends that helped him. This pattern went on for many centuries (and was later imported to the USA), where the owner of the land (the Crown) could remove an estate from one noble and give it to another. Many of the villages in Britain have one large mansion house with grounds, with tiny houses crowded up to the gates for the rest of the villagers to live in. People have been used to the hereditary ownership of land being concentrated in very few hands. The alternative would be villages where the houses and gardens are more equal in size.

Today many old mansions are open to the public to visit, and many of these are owned by outside organisations. This has turned out to be a valuable way to preserve open land for animals. Former deer parks, forests and arable land survive because they were once part of a wealthy family's estate. In the UK these properties are islands of almost-natural greenery in the midst of modern farmlands. They allow animals space to live while giving people the chance to live alongside of them. Animals bring life and activity to any area. Where there are a number of different types of animals there are droppings to carry plant seeds and feed a variety of insects. It is very far removed from a monoculture farm

Where are animals supposed to live in your world? Many of them are seen as pests or their access to water or breeding grounds is blocked by roads or farms. Somehow, by the end of your time on Earth you are going to have to learn to live with all living beings. We like that more people are aware that wood piles make a home for a greater number of insects and small animals, and that these are purposely left standing. When people feed wild birds there is pleasure in watching them and connecting to them through your heart. If no birds flew in to eat they would be sadly missed. Thinking of them as pests denies that animals and insects need something to eat and space to raise their young. There are many larger animals that are the prey of humans or simply denied the conditions they need to live. They range from the wildlife in the Rocky Mountains or great herds of animals on the plains of Africa, to a fox crossing a suburban garden. Some animals in National Parks in Africa are hunted to provide food for nearby families, but when the last animal is gone what will these people eat? In all of this we see your lack of understanding that you are a part of a larger world.

One of the reasons you do not live alongside animals is

that you don't really see them as beings in their own right. You have not been taught to appreciate them as unique individuals, instead you have been taught the opposite. They are often at your disposal to work for you, or to feed you. You are the only species to enslave others, and you do so out of ignorance. This is something you can remedy by getting to know animals as individuals. A rhinoceros carries birds on its back to pick up irritating bugs, and the relationship is symbiotic. A horse will carry a human on its back to enable you to become acquainted with all horses by getting to know one well. You are changed by your contact with other species, learning more about the world you live in, and the One who created all of you. If you accept each animal as an individual then you are closer to knowing the entire species. Most animals are cheerful and happy, and they are very aware of your sadness and moods.

Animals are willing to live with you domestically for one reason, and that is to teach you about themselves. They share a planet in community with all the other animals and insects except you, and they miss your company. They seek to interact with you to bring you into their world. You do not really see them or communicate with them outside of your house pets or farm animals. They have walked one path and you another, but you are all living here together at the same time to make it easier for you to learn from each other. Can you think of a better example of freedom than a bird in flight, or the rapid turns and movement of a school of fish? All animals were created by God and can show you an aspect of Him that you may otherwise miss, and learning about All There Is teaches you about yourself. Some of you are as free as a bird or swift and flexible as a fish, but it is easier to see this demonstrated in the animal kingdom.

Some animals are more highly evolved than you. Dolphins are an obvious example, and lizards a less obvious one. The point is that you can't tell who has evolved further because most of you aren't able to detect this kind of information right now. If you spent more time with animals as your teachers you would begin to learn more about your potential. This is not how you are taught to view animals, but if you did see them as equals, would it help you to see how you fit in with the other life on Earth?

One of the interesting lifetimes for a human is to be the servant of the horse; the one who cleans out the stable and brings the food. This is often the same person who did not learn to value horses in a previous life, but perhaps treated them the same way you treat your car. The servant of the horse usually has a great deal of love for horses and knows their different personalities. Animals have personalities because they are not carbon copies of each other, but individual bodies of an overall soul. Anyone who owns pets can tell you this; there is no need to fund scientific research for confirmation. Finding out information about pet animal species could be done by interviewing a series of owners and finding out what they have learned through experience.

Living with animals could be done very differently from the way you live now. You may think they would run from you, but your own pets do not run, and not all animals automatically run away when they see you. They run once they have learned you are a threat to them, or else they are like rabbits and everyone's prey. Animals eat other animals, but until the point of kill the prey animal has lived a free life and not been forced to live in a pen. Animals tend to see humans as another, albeit dangerous, animal. They would live alongside you if it were safe.

House pets volunteer to spend time with you on a one to one basis so you will learn to know and love them. Pets are very fond of their humans, as some of you will already know. People were not meant to live alone away from all other life, and you have fallen very far behind in learning about the other species on this planet. You are part of the web of life without recognising the web exists. The current game in progress for humanity has been an interesting experiment but we're not sure there is any more to learn by continuing in exactly the same manner. People have had plenty of chances to learn about themselves and who they are, but under the old conditions of the game progress has been slow. There are new conditions now, and a new Earth.

After the mistakes of Atlantis and little real human progress this rebirth of the Earth helps you to have a fresh start. You still have complete freedom to act, and we hope that when you decide to take an action you will consider all life around you, from birds to insects to bacteria. If you think of all life as another part of God, and therefore a tiny part of yourself, we hope you will choose to honour all living beings.

16

Turbulent Times Ahead

ONE OF the reasons the new Earth was reborn with a stronger sense of herself is to enter the final phase of this game. We wrote in *And I Saw A New Earth* that what was happening on this one planet has the potential to hasten the end of the universe, at the same force and speed as a rubber band snapping back. Among all the reasons we gave for this, one that was not mentioned was that this game had stagnated to the point where only a few humans were able to learn the important lessons. The Earth today is energetically shaking with pleasure, like a wet dog. One way to instigate change is to alter the surface the game is played on. Sometimes the game needs to change a little.

To take this one step further, how many times would you need to stick a pin in your arm before you learned it was a painful thing to do? You would learn the act caused damage and pain and would desist. There are many, many species that have already learned this type of lesson of cause and effect. These other species and the planet live here with you and it has been hard for them at times to wait for you to catch up. If that means you need to hurry and learn the same lessons that others have learned, then the right conditions for learning will be created. The Earth has changed her energy because she is a being of many capabilities and wisdom, and she has chosen carefully the quality of the new energy to help you learn. The overall amount of change in the planet is as slight to her as tying on a different coloured scarf; a filmy, minor change of her inner self. Earth has been a water planet, a gas planet and this beautiful land/water planet. She is only changing enough to help you progress to your stated goal. She is a soul who has chosen a physical form to meet the needs of her guests. It's solid land to you, and an energy hologram to her.

The Earth agreed to certain terms and conditions in order to accept the human soul group on Earth so they could learn once again who they are. (All previously explained in *Planet Earth Today*, *The Downfall of Atlantis*, *And I Saw A New Earth*.) She keeps the overall agreement but is able to change herself when she gets the chance. A complete rebirth with the help of the light boost from the Central Sun at the end of the last cycle was not possible, so she changed her insides. If you changed your insides people would start to notice the difference. Charles Dickens in *A Christmas Carol* wrote about Scrooge as a man who changed from being an angry miser to the kindest gentleman in town. Everyone took notice. The Earth has changed from a planet giving you a free rein to one who looks after her own interests alongside yours. Unhelpful pathways are being closed off. Some of these pathways led to terrible mass murders in the last century in country after country, from Stalin and Hitler to Pol Pot. Massacres do not need to be repeated on this scale and will continue to decrease.

Other pathways that are being choked off include killing animals as a recreational sport, allowing vast numbers of people to die in famines, and continuing to make profits from war and death. Everyone reading this will say they are all good things to stop, but there are many here who make a lot of money from war and the armaments industry. War is one of the world's largest industries along with food, oil and pharmaceuticals. Keeping people alive in famine countries is more than delivering bags of food. In many cases it is war that has destroyed local crops and the infrastructure to deliver clean water, food and health care. Some of the famine areas were beautiful once, but the cycles of the land work best when people and animals are few enough to move out of the area when drought begins. Not every part of the Earth is meant for large numbers of human beings to live on.

Think of a life where small groups of people walk in a pleasant land full of food. Would it really matter if you deserted your office buildings to walk with others and eating along the way? Why do you work for money if not to buy food and shelter? There are alternative examples to the way you live now, and one of them was the Native American tribes, and another the Aborigine of Australia. These were both mobile ways of living closely to the Earth. They actively cared for her and lived lightly on her surface. The Aborigine were few in number compared to the total size of Australia and they moved around out of the way of heat and drought. They balanced the energy of the places they visited because they still remembered how it was done in Atlantis and it was their pleasure to do so. It was only when the continent was settled by Europeans that immobility kept them trapped in one place.

Native Americans travelled north with their prey animals, and then south to avoid the worst of the winter weather. There were large winter camps where they met old friends and relations for storytelling and singing. If this sounds like a nice life, it was. There were some drawbacks and it wasn't perfect, but we think they were living a more pleasant life overall than many we see today.

The cornerstone of modern legal systems is private property. Letting go of this one concept would begin to unravel the basis of western economies. Life on Earth was meant to be free and easy, but once all land is privately owned it is neither. Everything we need for life is provided by the planet naturally yet money and ownership stand between each of us having an easy life in western culture. You have to pay for the food you eat, the water you drink and the ground you live on. Yet the person who originally decided they owned the land did not create it but simply declared it was theirs. In effect they stole it from the Earth and you, then by selling it to another human (or demanding taxes for it) they continued to profit from it. Is this fair to you?

The main point here is that economies will change and most of you will live through a period of turmoil. Your easiest way through to the light at the end of the tunnel is to let go of anything you don't really need to carry with you. You are not going to start living the lives of Native Americans or Aboriginals as that has already been done, but you are going to live in closer connection to the Earth, and that could be as simple as spending more time outside.

17

A New Way of Living

THE NEW ways of living with each other and the planet will encourage you to be happy. Happiness has to be at the forefront of your minds as everything is brought back into balance. There are genuine cases right now of people in business working themselves to an early death, or having a nervous breakdown. This should tell all of you that something is very wrong with the way you live your lives. Remember these personal tragedies and be glad that you are being helped to end this way of living. Above all, remember that you can swap money for happiness and that you are always looked after.

Money is a physical representation of the energy you build up to buy food and shelter. That is why people originally worked for money. Their energy was banked into money, and then that money could be saved up and spent. The current methods of speculation bypass this and have a very different feel to money that is accumulated. Speculation allows money to rise and fall quickly because it is not real in the same way. It is not the physical representation of anyone's work; it is a number on a computer. We look and wonder why anyone would settle for numbers on a computer when you could avoid the falseness of this and have something real. When we look at the energy of this type of addition to money it shimmers and is not really there, but money itself is still solid and real.

Being employed means you may have to work alongside other people at a job and be paid. There is more to working than being paid, and the best jobs include a sense of companionship and satisfaction that the day has been well spent. If you do not have this type of feeling at the end of the day then you may be in the wrong job. You can be happy at work by mixing with others and learning about yourself that way.

We may have made it sound like you will all be manual workers, but that is not what we mean. There are a large variety of jobs now, and there will continue to be a large variety in the future and your current employment may suit you just fine. The first generations on the new Earth that are alive right now will live through a period of rebalancing. The Earth will rebalance herself, societies, money and the way everyone lives. You were born for this, and many of you will see this life as exciting, where instead of pointless action you are able to be effective and make a difference. Most of you have not been happy with the status quo, and watched in frustration as your lives suffered under unfair systems and the planet was abused. Have you considered that you could work towards the changes you want? You have had so many changes imposed on you from the top down, it is not the same thing at all when you campaign for change and see positive results. This results in the kind of celebration you may have seen in movies when the sports team wins the game, or the political campaign wins the election. Working for change that is good for you makes you feel alive and purposeful. Worrying about change is a hangover from the old days when every change seemed to be more and more challenging. This time you will create the changes.

When we said you were born for this, out of the crowd of individual human souls waiting to be born on Earth, the others stood back and ushered you through to the front of the line. You were the souls with the qualities that were most needed for the task in hand. There are all age groups here, and some people have been working faithfully for sixty years or longer. Older people have been learning and teaching others while placing themselves where are most able to help. Now is the time for them to use their knowledge, experience and courage to help change the world. The generation in their twenties (and younger) are the ones to benefit from all this knowledge and effort. These young people came to restore balance, and they have the numbers to make a large difference.

Young people are energetic and tend to hold their views in black and white, right or wrong. The older generations can be the ones to see both sides of any story and this slows down their willingness to go all out and take action. Young people often have less to lose and less tolerance for injustice. They may not have been able to buy homes or find good jobs, and may feel excluded from the wealthy careers. Intolerance may sound like an undesirable trait, but can you think now why you would tolerate actions that hurt so many other people? Maybe you think you never do this, but if you support a system that causes people to live in unhappiness then by inaction you are assisting those who blight young lives.

How is this army of young people ever going to mobilise itself to cause change? Now we come to something else, a very real change in energy. In the past you tended to group together into ever larger organisations, but what if instead these organisations gently split apart and everything becomes smaller? Instead of large hospitals you could have small local ones or if instead of large companies you could have individual sections that break away while still trading.

If the energy changes to support smaller groups then large organisations cannot stand firm, and they will begin to collapse. Small groups of active young people will be able to take action to correct imbalances locally, and your town is a good place to start. It will also remove the need for national or international hierarchies. The distance between each person becomes less as they work together and they become closer to one another. No one will feel they can tell others to do something they are not prepared to do themselves.

Some of the work that needs to be done is cleaning up the messes made by previous generations. This doesn't sound at all fair, unless you take it back to one human soul split into individuals, and this generation of young people is doing exactly what it came here to do. It is a very determined group. They will be pushed into action by lack of living space, lack of jobs, and lack of opportunities. They will watch too many of their parents with nothing at the end of their lives of hard work. (There's a reason for everything; and the destitution of those who have worked for a lifetime will affect the way their children see the world.) Another form of action will be to simply walk away and not participate in the established economic systems. Older people may think the children of those who walked away will return to cities and fill in the employment gaps left by their parents, and everything will return to the way it was. That generation will not come and take a job just for the money, when there is no pleasure in it. Remember this is all about building a world where everyone lives happy and balanced lives.

The changes we spoke about in earlier sections of this book (and all three previous books) describe villages where everyone can live in a relaxed way. They live close enough to the Earth to feel her support, and will not feel the need to physically support themselves in standing tall. The support of the Earth is what you have all forgotten, the feeling that someone is cupping you in their hands so that you can't fall over and hurt yourself (watch the energy holding lambs as they gambol in the spring.) This support gives you strength, and the freedom to try new things. As long as you are aligned with the Earth and love you have her support. Her support is one hundred percent now, and that allows you the freedom to walk forward knowing that everything will turn out all right. The Earth gets stronger and more balanced every day.

18

Steps to a Balanced Earth

STEPS WILL be taken in the near future beginning the process of balancing the Earth, by balancing humanity. First, as we said earlier, there will be a change from very large organisations to smaller, more vibrant ones. The large global organisations are sitting in mid-air with no foundations or strength. In the past they have been complacent and were supported by the world's governments. Their day is fading and they will struggle in a way that smaller businesses will not. If a smaller business is being run by someone whose feet are on the new Earth, and is supported by the Earth, their energy will draw in business. As long as a business is grounded on the Earth it will have solidity. Most people will be glad to patronise local businesses where they know the owners, and when large businesses fade shopping will continue on a local level.

Changing this energy around big business is one of the key ways to alter your economies. You will not have to do anything yourselves to bring this about, it is part of the background energy of the new cycle. These businesses are top-heavy and unstable, and can topple easily. The decline of these big businesses will make space for something smaller to start, something of your own perhaps. There are many ways this can be done, and we want you to see that you will be going with the energy rather than against it, a little like walking with the wind at your back rather than into a stiff breeze. There are a lot of changes heading your way and there is no reason to delay any plans. The sooner you put plans of your own into action the better.

Another change will be alterations in the Earth itself through flooding, earthquakes, volcanoes, tsunamis, etc. What can we say about this – don't build or buy a house in a flood plain, on a vulnerable coastline, on the slope of a volcano? You already know these are not good places for people to live. We really want to emphasise the coastlines right now. They have been fairly stable for a long time, and some people own beautiful homes looking out to sea. Their stability is about to change, and although they will remain lovely places to visit, your coastlines are vulnerable. Not just from large waves this time, but with parts of various coastlines breaking off and falling into the sea. There will be new coastlines over time. Turbulent is a good word for what is going to be happening on the coasts of many nations as the Earth resettles itself. The correction to the Earth's axis will have a big effect on the world's coastlines.

The Earth has always reshaped herself over the millennia, and there have been ice-ages and warm periods. These affect water by holding it frozen in ice or releasing it into the oceans and lakes. You have noticed global warming and some of you are worried, especially the millions of people in low-lying countries like Bangladesh or the Maldives. In past ages the Earth could make a little adjustment without affecting millions of people as they did not live in those areas; there were only a few who lived close enough in harmony with her to sense what was coming and walk away, and resettling themselves elsewhere. Now humanity has a problem that is theirs alone, which is that your population is so large and inflexible that many people are living in vulnerable locations. There are a million people living on the side of an active volcano in Central Africa. They wouldn't be living there if there were anywhere else for them to live. How are you going to help these millions of people world-wide? They are an extension of your own soul and an opportunity for you to learn about sharing and compassion. This will be one of the first challenges for humanity as the planet changes.

After a certain number of years people will have had the chance to connect to others and see a part of their own soul looking back out of stranger's eyes. Then you will be able to move forward together, and sharing the better land on the planet will not seem a hardship, it will seem normal and right. You will have to realise that you all are one at some time, and your kindness to refugees will help you take a little step in the right direction. If you were a refugee you would like someone to help you, and some of the unpredictable events in the coming years could make a great many of you homeless. It's started already with flooding around the world, and will escalate over time. This is another reason why flexibility and not overburdening yourselves with possessions will help you move quickly out of the way of trouble. There won't be geological problems everywhere, but the Earth will be readjusting some of her pressure points, and the axis will be straightening up. Water moves more quickly than earth, making flooding one of the more immediate problems.

Right now you may be thinking that there will be many people dying, and it will be terrible! We're not talking about millions of people dying, although some will die in these catastrophes. But the numbers of people dying afterwards will be reduced by opening your hearts and borders to those who need help. Borders keep you divided from each other, and are fairly inflexible. Do borders in their present forms serve humanity as a whole? We said this was a human problem of overpopulation, but it also presents an opportunity for growing closer together. There may be some who are appalled that they may be asked to share with others, but most people will come forward to help. They will think of treating others the way they would like to be treated themselves, and they will do everything they can to assist. There is enough to go around for everyone on the planet right now if it were shared out more equitably. You won't have to live in primitive shacks, but those in shacks could live in nicer homes and have enough to eat. Rather than a catastrophe, this could be seen as a great opportunity to learn to live together.

After you have learned to live more closely with others and with loving kindness, then you have completed that lesson. Once the need for one lesson is gone another will present itself. This time when you deal with new circumstances you will address it from a completely different point of view. Instead of 'us' and 'them' it will just be 'us.' That will be a major change for humanity; rebalancing years of separation in a species. Where wars and genocide have taken place there will be respect and love again for all people. This step is necessary for your greater human soul to ascend.

Rebalancing the Earth will also affect your fossil energy use. Part of the effort to heat and cool yourselves is because you have moved out to the margins of your habitable world. From the Inuit to desert dwellers (Saudi Arabia to Arizona) people have moved out of the centre to exploit niches in hunting and food. Humanity will still visit these wonderful areas, prime examples of the variety on your living planet, but by residing in more temperate areas and by the design of your dwellings you can reduce the amount of energy you need. Will there be fewer people? Yes, and you are peaking now around seven billion. The reasons for over-population are already falling behind you into your past. Population reduction will come about in a natural way as people start to have smaller families. There will be many reasons why there are smaller families around the world, from lack of fear that the children will not live to grow up, to not wanting to struggle to find food for so many mouths. It will take place over a few generations. People just won't see the need to reproduce themselves in such numbers. This corner has already been turned, energetically.

Balancing the Earth is not up to you to accomplish. Your job is to hang on while she changes and to learn all about love. The challenges you go through as your world changes will force you to balance your own lives and your own soul. As you balance the way the human soul lives on the Earth's surface, you will help to balance her physical form with her inner energy. She's been holding still so long that she is going to give a shake now and then with the resultant tremors, and the biggest change right now is the way she is shaking energetically. This caused large cracks to appear in her energy shell. By March 2013 that shell had dissolved and Earth was open everywhere to the rest of the universe, except inside man-made buildings. The planet and all of us who live here are being bombarded by life and reconnected to a universe that fizzes with activity.

In the past the Earth agreed to a set of conditions to help humanity learn about who they are as a small part of God. Most planets will completely enclose a learning game like this so there is no outside interference and it can progress as desired. Due to the human blindfold that keeps the higher dimensions veiled, this game has taken a very long time. Earth has been in a sturdy cocoon of silence while the rest of the universe has been in constant communication while learning about life together. She is moving the game forward by removing the protective shell and you will have to move with her. It will feel like a whole new game for most of you; and very few of you are expecting this to happen, or have any idea of what this could mean. It could be as dramatic for you as a butterfly crawling out of a chrysalis, turning from a caterpillar into a free-flying beauty.

An Earth open to the universe will import knowledge about so many new ideas. Old and useless ideas will still be here, but new ideas will spring forth about how life could be lived in better ways. Alternatives will be put forward that many will embrace, and these will crash straight into the old ideas that have been in place for so long. Adhering to the past, and trying to live as one did in the past will eventually become a dead end. For those of you who want to carry on with your lives, and not everyone will want to, you will find that you live through so many changes that change becomes the norm. You will have adapted to continuous change and that is the goal in this universe. You are then very close to living without effort, flowing from one event to another.

When we talk about living with the flow of the universe we mean that energy is never still, but matter is quite solid. You will be changing from the solidity of matter to the flow of energy and become like quicksilver, quick to move and change direction by following the way of least resistance. As you move from day to day you will follow your path, let's say as a horse trainer, and you will be brought into contact with others just at the moment they are looking for someone to train their horses. You have your next job and it is all so effortless. You want to move to a larger house to raise a family and the perfect house comes along for you, while someone comes to take your old home at the same time. Today you would say someone is lucky and that everything works out great for them. What do you think luck is, other than the ability to be in the right place at the right time? All of you will be lucky in the end. This could take a few years, but with the Earth's shell is gone everything could happen very fast if you allow it to.

In life there are some people who resist change with all their might, and others that accept it and move on. When change comes along irregardless, both kinds of people will change but it will be easier and less painful for some. They will move forward while the others are trying to hold still, and in the end the movers will be far ahead looking back to see where the others are. Their reward for letting go is living life easily, and trusting that what they need will come to them at the right time. That is how the rest of the universe understands life, as something that has love and connection woven through it. You will be bombarded with this knowledge and it will help you to let go and move forward. When you are interconnected, the person who is looking for help will meet just the right person. Right now when some of you trust the universe to look after you it does, but your available pool of other people to cooperate with is not so large and there can be a time lag. One day it will include all of you and you will be like a pinball machine bouncing from one person you need straight on to the next. Other people will find you in the same way, and you will all be moving at once. Those who refused to stand up and walk forward will be the first to fall away.

Life is not meant to be scary and impossible. You are not

meant to wonder where your next meal will come from or if your house will be washed away and you'll be left homeless. Life is about ease and pleasure, company and joy. If you find yourself in this position, you don't have to do anything else. The purpose of letting go of old beliefs and all that go with them is to arrive at that point and live happily. Perhaps you can arrive years before other people, and be happy for longer than they are. It will take acceptance that once you have landed in the perfect place for you, there may be an even more perfect place and you could be swept off again. Notice we did not say you struggled off again, but nothing stands still and there are many lovely things to experience in a beloved universe.

You have not lived like this before on this planet; this will be new. When we say you have learned certain lessons and don't need to repeat them, it's because you will be too busy learning about change and flow, and the happiness you can find when you trust and let go. This is a lesson, and you will be given time to learn how to trust and let go. There are very few people that learn in an instant, and most lessons require some practice. Being alive is a chance to practice lessons and learn while having fun. If your life isn't fun to live, then join with others and change what you can. You are the current generation on a new planet and everything you do matters now. You have a chance to lift the burden of unhappiness that has descended on you and the Earth.

Scientific Discoveries and Changes in Travel 2013 Onwards

19

The End of Old Technology

TRAVEL and scientific discoveries are linked, of course. Humanity will be taught science by the outer universe and scientists will no longer do all of the teaching themselves. We're not even sure that scientists will notice everything that's new, but we don't see the next developments coming from inside the current research centres and establishments. There are already many new discoveries coming from creative outsiders, especially the young people who use computers so effectively. Since the time of the Renaissance, scientists have been exploring the physical world, with the old world they explored now gone. Many scientific theories put forward as fact in the past were later disproved and quietly dropped, but some discoveries remain true. Humanity has been so slow to learn! You have barely scratched the outer surface of knowledge whilst spending so much time and money on experimentation. Your discoveries have for the most part gone into industry but there are many ways to use the information already in existence, and there is little point in discovering new information unless it is put to good use. The scientific establishment's requirement for double-blind testing has held you back; it only applies to part of the existing accumulation of knowledge.

Humanity has been on Earth for such a long time now that your science has fallen quite far behind the rest of the universe. Other planets hosted games that finished more quickly and made use of information shared inside the individual soul groups and between the species. They no longer use science for warfare and killing, but are more concerned with everyday life and healing. Do not look for the universe to teach you more methods of killing yourselves, nor new ways to pollute the planet. They went through those phases long ago and the methods you use now will suffice. It is old technology to dig up all the coal or drain all the oil and gas from a planet. In the future you may expect to live the same way as you do today but with greater simplicity and ease. Until you see the goal of life as happiness and not as quantities of possessions you will continue to be surprised by the new changes.

Other planet's populations have been working toward knowing themselves, and found it easiest when they work together. Their souls have been focussing on relationships and co-existence. Many varieties of games have been played on other planets, as before the start of every new game ground rules are laid down. The planet provides the conditions for a new game, while the souls incarnate and begin their lives. Some souls choose to be as close as a school of fish, and move and think as one. The boundaries created by their physical bodies barely impinge on their collective consciousness. Others have an ever looser connection right across the spectrum until reaching humanity where you are so disconnected that you don't realise you are one soul. You all crave love and connection to another person whether mother, father or partner. This is entirely natural and every time it happens it makes you feel happy. Love makes you happy, and hate and disdain do not.

In your great experiment of loneliness and separation on Earth you established that complete isolation from other people doesn't make you happy, and that the absence of happiness means life is tolerated but not enjoyed. If you understood that it is your connection to others that makes you happy you would jettison everything you own just to be with them.

20

What Happens on Other Planets?

O N ANOTHER planet a similar soul to you would be finding out how to be happy by concentrating on those around them. Everyone you meet is a mirror of yourself, for are you not all human? When you look into a mirror and see something you don't like, you change your appearance. You have mastered the concept that you are the only one who can change yourself when it comes to a glass mirror, but the same applies when you are faced with another human being and their actions. The glass mirror shows you the outside, but your fellow beings show you the inside. This is where every personality trait that you don't like in another person is one you already tend to exhibit. That is exactly why you find it so painful to see someone else's behaviour at times. Inside you know that you are exactly the same, but you don't like yourself or the other person who shows you that you could be better. Once you realise this, and there are many of you that do, you have the difficult task of changing your insides. Usually what happens is that people don't understand that they behave in much the same way, and they get angry with another's behaviour. The angrier they get, the closer that person is mirroring their own personality.

The human mirror contains the hardest lessons that life will ever show you, and requires the deepest knowledge of yourself to correct. Mirroring is the mechanism for soul growth in this universe; and the pain of digging deep and changing yourself is at times worked on alone. Fellow humans are gifts that reflect you back to yourself. If you feel trapped for years with someone you dislike, the other person is very good at showing you the parts of yourself you like the least. If you didn't need them to reflect back to you they wouldn't be in your life. Leaving an unpleasant co-worker or partner will often bring that same type of personality right back into your lives. On the other hand, when you are through with that version of yourself in the universal mirror it is easy to move on to the next lesson.

Marriage is a steep learning curve. When two people partner each other, they do so to mirror the other person's deepest soul. Once a relationship has run it course this mirror will have stopped working, and the learning can continue with another partner. If in the coming years you see fewer marriages and more arrangements that are new to you, it will be because humans are learning about themselves in new ways. What has existed for many years may vanish very quickly. In the future we see you living more communally, and with more shared spaces mixed with areas of privacy. The single family home will fade from use.

Some people spend their lifetime as some kind of a therapist (not just mind, but body as well) and notice that everyone who comes to them is showing them something they need to look at for themselves and heal. Therapists have chosen to work hard on themselves in this lifetime. Perhaps you don't need to do this, but you will still be faced by people who make you angry until you acknowledge to yourself that even you can behave in exactly the same way. Then forgive yourself and move on. When it comes to knowing yourself you have no deadline, and no lack of lifetimes for learning. If you see it as a game and an adventure to learn more about yourself, and regard each setback as a learning experience, then you are rediscovering the purpose of your life here. For example, when you realise you do not treat others the way you would like to be treated yourself, then you can break that pattern and move on to another lesson. Being stuck in a situation can mean you have more to learn on the subject, or even that a new lesson around standing up for yourself and walking away is being offered. Rather than second guess what you need to learn in every situation put your energy into having experiences and living. The lessons will come at the right time.

On other planets everything that's learned by one being is combined into the greater soul consciousness more quickly. Souls are either like bees that share telepathically while alive, or they share information after death across the entire soul. Souls are able to learn a lot very quickly that way. Imagine if you died and learned everything that each of seven billion people learned during their lives, and then had a new life where you could apply it all. You would learn very fast. The universe has existed for a long time, and there have been countless examples of learning like this already. You share some information while alive, as for example in this book, but when you are reborn you pick up with the same knowledge you had in your last life. Humanity separated into physical beings and never shared what they learned in life once dead. Many lives are spent reliving certain difficult lessons until you really understand them, making your progress very slow. Seven billion human bodies may seem like a huge amount of souls on the planet, but there are still a vast number of individual souls that are not incarnate at this time.

Souls without bodies are carefully watching everything that

happens, and most of them are making plans for their future. They consider which circumstances and people could help them learn the lessons they don't yet understand. Take a murderer for example. Until that person has murdered someone, been murdered, been the parent, spouse, child or sibling of someone killed, and until they know all about the emotions surrounding murder they will continue to explore murder. You've all been there yourselves, or will be before you know all there is to know about being human. For this reason it will help if you can hold back on judging people, as it could have been you in the past. There are countless ways to know yourself.

21

Spirit Guides

W HEN YOU are dead you can still learn by watching, or as some of you have found, by being a spirit guide. The ascended masters and mistresses are well known spirit guides, but there are many guides who have not yet ascended. There are far more people working their way up the ladder of knowledge than the few who have reached the top and ascended as an individual. By guiding living people on their pathways some spirit guides learn by being more closely involved with their problems and emotions. If you are on a spiritual pathway while alive you have one or more guides. If you are not consciously on a spiritual pathway you probably don't have any spirit guides, and if you concentrate on looking just for the guides around a living person you will see that not everyone has them. The best way to get your first guide is to ask the spirit world for help, and they will come instantly.

The first strata of guides will have a lower vibrational level than the ascended master level and therefore these can be more easily contacted. People who practice Reiki or another healing modality will be supported by the Reiki energy when in contact with their guides. If a person is not a channel the human must be guided by nudging them in certain directions and hoping they will take the hint. After a while people's guides may change, some may drop out and others join in. They have the guides most suited to them at that moment.

As a person's vibrational level climbs they must have practiced their Reiki (or similar healing) or channelling to maintain their own level high enough to meet the vibration of those who come to help them. By the time one is guided by an ascended master the vibrational level must have risen high enough and be held long enough for it to be possible. This is not something that happens overnight, but by practicing every day. One can move from being nudged along a pathway to hearing and seeing more information over the passage of time. Channelling for a long period of time is tiring as it the concentration and vibrational level must be kept higher that it would normally be in everyday life.

Channelling is something that humans naturally do, but it is unused by most people. Usually a person will get a "hunch" or their intuition tells them what to do or where to go. This can feel like a gentle nudge. As angels we are working hard at times to influence people into a direction that is helpful to them. We do this because we exist in timeless space and we can see various possibilities and outcomes, some more positive than others that will lead to greater happiness. Once you are travelling on your pathway you will pass crossroads with choices, and the choices are different each time. We try to guide you towards happiness, but the choice is yours. When you feel that a certain path is calling to you, even if it appears difficult, chances are we are nudging you. If you decide to carry on as you are, we will keep nudging you whenever the opportunity arises.

Sometimes on Earth opportunities come around again in a slightly different form, and events will squeeze you to go towards your highest good. If you have reached the point where your choices are narrowing and you feel pushed to go in a certain direction, then is the time to make an effort to change.

Sometimes following the easiest path will not take you where you ultimately want to go, and at times it is necessary to focus on what you want, rather than how you are going to get it. Once you have chosen a pathway and made the necessary changes you may find you are walking easily on it. Making the change is hard, but once you have done that the new pathway can be smooth. Changing is the hardest part.

Pathways are waiting for each one of you to take you forward. Once you commit to move you will find the pathway is wide and level, and may even be similar to one of those electric walkways you find in large airports. If you find yourself on one of those it is because you have chosen to trust life and the universe, and you are ready to receive effortlessly all the good things that are being offered to you. You are not used to receiving good things on trust yet. You will become more in tune all the time with the outer universe and life.

22

Rewired by the Universe

THE EARTH has existed for millennia under a blanket of *time*. She was a planetary ball inside an energy shell, and the shell kept her games private and intact by utilising time. These games can't be interfered with by any passing being who decides to stop and see what is happening down there. One of the first things to happen on the new Earth in January 2013 was this energy shell cracking and dissolving, and by spring 2013 it was gone. This exposed people to the timeless universe and allowed the planet to extend her 'antennae' out to rejoin the busy life that exists there. As the planet extends her feelers out to link up, people do the same. The difference is that some people will be ready to extend many antennae outwards, and others will extend only a few. The people that did not choose to come to the new Earth with the others will be aware of what is happening on the inside, but they will not participate. Many other people will make a personal connection to the universe for the first time.

Reiki is Universal Life Force energy, and those who have practiced their Reiki over the years will have spent time already connecting to the universe on a daily basis. But Reiki is not the same energy that we are referring to here, as Reiki involves love (I love myself enough to practice my Reiki) and connecting to the healing Reiki energy whether by treating others or themselves. Other healers who are practicing what they have been taught, for example, in Sufism, Spiritual Healing, Shamanism, etc. are also spending time connecting to healing energy while practicing their modality. One of the reasons you have been given all these different ways of healing with energy is to encourage you to practice at least one of them. People make different choices depending on their personalities and there are plenty of healing methods to choose from. These are the people who are sending up a lot of antennae now; they were ready for the shell to dissolve and were already reaching a healing antenna through to the universe.

Does this mean that no one will benefit from practising healing anymore? Being connected to the universe will strengthen and heal you, but if you are used to being a healer in this life you are needed as much as ever. The universe has the potential to heal your bodies and minds through balance but people will barely be able to adjust to this level of change without help in their current lifetimes. Newborn babies will be different, having been born onto the new Earth. People will need healing to adjust to the bombardment of 'home' energy, for the universe is your home, and to the construction of their new antennae. Those people with one or two antennae will be helped and connected slightly more than they were before. Those who have sent up a number of antennae are busy being rewired into the entire universe. These people will find it much easier to walk forward for the remainder of their lives with greater intuition and understanding. You will be basing your movements and your lives on what you are absorbing through your increased connection.

23

Scientific Discoveries through Symbols

INFORMATION from the entire universe has been entering Earth in the form of symbols. Each symbol is a shorthand description of an idea, happening or thing. Most of you can't see these symbols but they can grow and expand into every direction and provide manufacturing blueprints to make things that have never before been seen on Earth. This information is already here. There are many symbols here now that teach about caring for others: medicine, care of the elderly, care of animals, and most importantly the care of the planet. You live on the planet and need her to be healthy to be healthy yourselves. Your medicine does the best it can, but you are still treating cancer by using poisonous chemicals or life threatening radiation to kill cells. Imagine a safer way to kill cancer, clean and easy surgery, cleaning out arteries so the heart stays strong, and sight and hearing restored. Old age could be comfortable and active right up until death along with help for the brain and weak bones. Animals could be released from pens and allowed to live happier lives, and the planet could see an end to drilling, mining, fracking and nuclear power. Nuclear fission is too intensely hot for her.

Another group of symbols is about creating warm buildings and travel. Currently you are travelling by primitive means and by burning something you pumped or dug from the Earth. Even travelling by electricity involves a power station fuelled by coal, gas or nuclear power. On other planets personal fliers are not powered by these methods, and you now have that information here on Earth. The symbols arrive and settle onto people who are apt to use them, and they are slowly drawn inwards to rest in their hearts. Once the symbol is accepted there the idea will work its way out at the right time and someone will be inspired to make something completely different. This creative use of technology has been relatively rare in the past, but it will be happening everywhere in the coming years. You have completely new technology arriving now to help you begin to catch up to life on the rest of the planets.

Talking about scientific symbols is fairly straightforward, but we hope you will have taken on board the other changes in society. Society is very complex and touches everyone in a heart-felt way that science does not. There are new symbols dealing with change in society. You can accept that things will change and not let it disturb you, or you could oppose new developments.

24

Travel

HOW WOULD you like to do your travelling from place to place? Buoyant personal fliers are common on planets elsewhere, they skim above the ground and park tethered to trees or rooftops. Giant spaceships have been developed for interstellar travel and visiting. These are part of a universe where each life form is valued and wants to become acquainted with each other. The closest you have to this at the moment is nature documentaries where you explore the Earth's animals and insects. Imagine when far in the future you have learned all about your own planet, and you want to make friends with everything across the galaxy. Interstellar travel will be used to come closer to others in your galaxy. Your horizons will become larger and Earth becomes the place you go back to when you return home. You will feel that although all these other species are not human, they are also part of God and worthy of love and respect. The symbols are already on Earth for these space ships. Because they exist elsewhere, the blueprints are here now. The universe can't become whole unless all life grows closer together.

You are near the end of this universe, in the last 3% or so of its long lifespan. As the planet with one of the most backward populations you will catch up to the others very quickly. The rebirth of the Earth in December 2012 began the snap back towards the light for the universe. You will remain a backward planet until you change away from valuing money and prestige.

Interstellar travel is something you think about now as taking decades and light years. Because other planets have already discovered the technology to move more quickly, you will benefit from their work. It takes very little time to travel within your galaxy, at the moment others travel for about ten Earth days to go from one side to another. The experience is a little like taking an ocean cruise, where the journey is part of the pleasure. In order to do this economically the fuel source has been reduced to the light available from stars. Pure light holds more energy than anything else, and by swinging past star after star the ships keep moving. The storage of light on board is minimal, only enough to make sure the ship isn't stranded between stars. Carrying heavy and explosive fuel on your rocket ships has limited your scope; you feel you must be full of fuel before you head to the moon or Mars. By using pure light the ships absorb the vibration of light which we angels feel as love. These are ships powered by love. If you can power space ships on love, what else can be powered by it and what changes could be expected?

Looking into telescopes you can see galaxy after galaxy and it does require the storage of fuel to travel across the dark spaces that exist between them. This has brought about a separate development in travel, one where the consciousness travels but the body stays behind. In the past there were years of sending fuel-laden spaceships to other galaxies, and sometimes these were stranded in the darkness never to be seen again. In the end the consciousness of the visitor could visit anywhere they pleased for free, but their interaction with the locals was impossible. It was a case of viewing only.

What happened next was that telepathy increased, and many learned the trust needed to accept a visitor and speak mind to mind. This is used at the moment to exchange information through intergalactic conferences where new ideas are discussed or demonstrated. It has been of interest to scientists, to anthropologists and historians, who like to find out about other planets and their populations. We like it because it brings different beings closer together. If anyone wants to physically travel to another galaxy they usually do so only when invited. In Earth years it could take between one and two years onboard a ship to reach another galaxy.

Travelling and leaving your body behind is common outside of Earth. In the rest of the universe it is how you jump forward or backward in time. We see that you are working on time-travel on Earth, but you want to take your physical body with you, and it is far easier to travel using your consciousness only. Your consciousness is the part of you that is alive, and your physical body houses the consciousness. If you have ever seen a dead body you know this already. For time and space travel it is common to leave your body in a chair or bed while you visit and most visits are fairly short. Because scientists insist on taking physical bodies you deny there are already people on your planet that practice time travel without them. Your world is both more complex and simple than you realise. From time travel to intergalactic travel is a short step.

In the beginning you will use the new technology to travel outwards and discover new planets. Some people are already talking about visits to Mars and setting up colonies there, but humanity is handicapped by only seeing three dimensions, or maybe five in the near future. The Martian civilisation is not handicapped in this way. Where we, and some of you, see a planet that is settled with beings the rest of you see emptiness. There are no empty planets. Not seeing the higher dimensions is a real set-back for you. Mars could be the first planet you visit and the locals exist across all twelve dimensions, they will see you coming and you will not be able to see them.

Do you see now why you may have been shielded here on Earth by the energy of linear time? You devised a game where you were blind to the higher dimensions. You live with smaller animals that see further than you, but are not trying to destroy you. Your game was perfectly designed to achieve an end, and the other planets work in exactly the same way. They are only in contact with one another through choice, and have designed games that include some very advanced challenges to their self-knowledge. Your own game sounds simpler, but has had so many complications over time that you have learned more than many other souls with more complex games. It was in no one's interest to interrupt this game unnecessarily.

One of the ways you were protected by time on your planet was due to its incredible slowness. From elsewhere it looked like you were moving in extra-slow motion. If anyone wanted to interfere on Earth they had to move just as slowly as you do, and it limited the damage humanity could cause elsewhere through wearing the blindfold. Fewer events took place on Earth over the years because of the slowness of time. This was important because you were unable to see all the entities of darkness, or the darkness in men's hearts. Any angel of darkness that took up residence on Earth moved at your speed and you had your normal amount of time to circumvent them. You have been sealed in here for what seems like a very long time; but this came to an end in the spring of 2013.

The break up of the outer shell of energy around the Earth was caused by the Earth's higher dimensional shaking after her rebirth, allowing life here to be part of the universe for the first time since this game began. Readers of this book may partially adapt to the change, but young children and babies will be quite different, like little star children. They won't find it hard to cope with the changes that are coming; it will seem like their normal world. Neither will they live behind veils as you have in the past. The people alive on the planet now are the ones to teach them, take care of the planet on their behalf and set in place protections to the environment so the Earth is still a world of beauty by the time these children grow up. You will still have purpose and meaning to your lives, and one day when you die you can come back and live here as one of those star children with the wisdom of the universe shining in your eyes.

It is the nature of this Earthly game to be balanced on a knife edge, and the greatest amount of learning takes place under these conditions. Humanity ran a huge risk when it chose to be blindfolded to the higher dimensions, but you are still here and still learning. We think the human soul will make it to ascension with the rest of life on Earth but you can't relax and assume someone else will cause it to happen. You as an individual will make it happen because only you have control over your own life. The only way to achieve ascension is by pursuing happiness at every opportunity.

Books by Candace Caddick

In 2009 the Archangels wanted to write a channelled book about the Earth, and help us to see the reality of the world we live on. *Planet Earth Today* shows a sentient planet of incredible beauty, and a human soul of light. I channelled this book by six Archangels, which was a combination of them explaining and me asking questions. *Planet Earth Today* is the first book of a trilogy including *The Downfall of Atlantis* and *And I Saw a New Earth* that the Archangelic Collective wrote about the coming years, as they have much to teach us. The contents of their books are always relevant to what is happening now.

There is a single story of humanity, a golden book like a long scroll and the three books have been taken from here and typed up. I felt that as long as I was learning new information when writing, information that I couldn't begin to make up, I was on track as an accurate channel. I watched the flow of golden words enter the computer each time until it was the last page of the book. After that my daughter and I checked and checked that I had written it correctly, each paragraph and line examined to see if the golden energy ran through it steadily or if it wavered indicating that it was not quite accurate. Only when we were happy was a section considered complete. Later sometimes I would add more clarity to a section, as my own understanding improved and I could put in more detail. I channel using a combination of sound and sight, and where it is written the best I have been writing down their exact words.

Planet Earth Today

The first book gives background information on the roles of Earth and the human soul in the universe. Life is experienced so that they can know themselves and learn why they are alive. Humanity wished to live on Earth wearing a blindfold; they could see neither the higher dimensions or connect to their greater human soul. This led to great loneliness and separation as you began to play the hardest game ever conceived. The Archangel of Darkness presents his point of view of humanity on Earth, and the Archangels of Light: Ariel, Esmariel, and Hophriel write with techniques to take you forward with hope.

This book serves as the introduction to the trilogy as it takes place before the other two books in time, and the information there about the planet or Atlantis is not repeated in any other book. However, each book stands alone and can be read individually.

ISBN 978-0-9565009-0-8

'The clearest message for me is: We have to act now! This book suggests gentle, effective ways to make small changes in our daily lives and help secure a bright future for humanity and for the Earth that hosts us.'

DEB HOY, *Editor Touch Magazine. UK*
(available from www.reikiassociation.org.uk)

'This clearly written, cleanly channelled book is a must for anyone willing to look at the bigger picture of Earth's history and humanity's part in her destiny.'

KRISTIN BONNEY, *Reiki Master UK*

The Downfall of Atlantis

In the story of humanity on Earth, the time spent living and learning on Atlantis cannot be ignored. During those long years the darkness gathered around human beings, and science developed a heartless approach. There were slaves made of combinations of animals and people and ultimately cloning to keep the wealthy and important alive indefinitely. Cloning was the final crack in the system that led to ruin and the end of Atlantis.

Those who refused to go along with the new science escaped the end and settled on the surrounding land masses forming the new post-Atlantean civilisations. The Atlantean influence is explored in the cultures of Africa, Egypt, Britain and Celtic Europe, North, Central and South America. They learned much from these people in return.

Their civilisation remained intact for a long time in Britain because of the ancient sites of power at Avebury, Stonehenge and Glastonbury Tor. When the Shadow in the East pushed westwards into Europe the light of these venerable societies vanished until only (the now mythical) King Arthur and Merlin were left to protect the Earth from darkness. Their story explains the true significance of the great stone circles, and how we came to forget the real story of Arthur and the sacrifices he made to destroy the invading armies. The connection in a straight line between Atlantis, post-Atlantean civilisations, King Arthur and the Time of Legends is explored so we can remember those things we have forgotten, and not repeat past mistakes.

ISBN 978-0-9565009-1-5

Books available from online retailers.

What they said about *The Downfall of Atlantis:*

'I love this book! It made me feel so at home. I was always drawn to Atlantis but could never find enough reliable information that would help me to connect to that past. This book presents Atlantis as if you are physically there and going through its history day by day. This account is alive as well as informative to the last detail. Absolutely amazing! Once I opened the book I literally could not put it down and practically inhaled it. I could read it over and over again and it still feels fresh as if I've never read it before. I can't quite explain it and to be honest don't really want to. I just love it!'

M. ODINTSOVA-BAYLES, *reader*

'What I love most about the information being shared is that there is practical guidance for how we humans can live in harmony not only with each other but with planet Earth as well. ... The strongest message of the book is that one person can make a difference in the world and that we each need to be that person. These are voices that need to be heard above the din of "modern" society.'

K. TLUSTY-RISSMAN, *reader*

And I Saw A New Earth

Humanity is entering its golden years, when you begin to live as you always intended when you came to Earth. It will be like breathing for the first time, the sweet fresh air that is real life filled with joy, truth and clear-sightedness. *And I Saw A New Earth* is a channelled book about light, written by those who have ascended in wisdom and understanding and wish to help during a time of rapid change.

During 2012 the Earth received wave after wave of light, enough light to change the way you relate to each other, enough light to show you the lies that have kept you from living in joy. By December the rebirth of Earth herself took place filled with the energy of Spring and fresh beginnings. Humanity can use this energy to remove the institutions that failed to work, and restore the balance between work and play. 2012 ended the world you know: one of gross inequality and lack of hope. The coming years give you the chance to build societies of love and fairness, and leave behind the institutions that failed you.

And I Saw a New Earth is written to reassure you that you can trust your intuition and your hearts, and that your real future lies ahead for you to enjoy. Humanity has one of the most important roles in the future of the universe.

ISBN: 978-0-9565009-2-2

Books available from online retailers

What they said about *And I Saw A New Earth:*

'Although this book is an extremely 'easy read', it is one I felt needed to be taken slowly and steadily to be able to fully digest all the fascinating and encouraging information within its pages. With each chapter being devoted to a particular subject, this book answers many questions whilst opening up new perspectives for the reader to explore. One of the best channelled works I have seen – it has certainly given me much on which to ponder.'

JOAN OSBORNE, *Paradigm Shift Magazine* March 2013

'...The book can provide an understanding of why our lives may seem busy, sped-up and challenging and may draw our attention to a gentle loving energy that is seeping through amid the chaos....For a dose of optimism, openings to love, and for practical ways to use Reiki amid the change, reach for a copy now...'

Reiki Touch Magazine Oct 2012

About the Author

I am a teaching Reiki Master who studied for ten years with my Master prior to initiation in the Usui Shiki Ryoho system of Reiki. During the course of the twenty years I've been practicing my own Reiki, my ability to channel became clearer and stronger until a few years ago I realised I was able to see the world around me in a way that others did not. My efforts as I worked with my own archangelic guides as a channel was always to unblock and be clear, with no preconceptions of what they may say next; to stand well back and just watch and listen.

Before learning Reiki I trained as an economist, worked inside the United States Congress in Washington D.C. as a legislative assistant, and retrained as a nutritionist in the UK. I found it interesting when channelling this book about the future that it combines Reiki, nutrition and economics into one long story.

If you want to read more from the Archangels and other beings of light, I write a regular channelled blog at:

www.candacecaddick.com

Lightning Source UK Ltd.
Milton Keynes UK
UKOW042257260513

211262UK00001B/20/P

9 780956 500939